Forensic Accounting

*What the World's Best Forensic Accountants Know
– That You Don't*

© **Copyright 2018**

All Rights Reserved. No part of this book may be reproduced in any form without permission in writing from the author. Reviewers may quote brief passages in reviews.

Disclaimer: No part of this publication may be reproduced or transmitted in any form or by any means, mechanical or electronic, including photocopying or recording, or by any information storage and retrieval system, or transmitted by email without permission in writing from the publisher.

While all attempts have been made to verify the information provided in this publication, neither the author nor the publisher assumes any responsibility for errors, omissions or contrary interpretations of the subject matter herein.

This book is for entertainment purposes only. The views expressed are those of the author alone, and should not be taken as expert instruction or commands. The reader is responsible for his or her own actions.

Adherence to all applicable laws and regulations, including international, federal, state and local laws governing professional licensing, business practices, advertising and all other aspects of doing business in the US, Canada, UK or any other jurisdiction is the sole responsibility of the purchaser or reader.

Neither the author nor the publisher assumes any responsibility or liability whatsoever on the behalf of the purchaser or reader of these materials. Any perceived slight of any individual or organization is purely unintentional.

Contents

INTRODUCTION 1

CHAPTER 1 – WHAT IS FORENSIC ACCOUNTING? 3
    LITIGATION SUPPORT 3
    INVESTIGATION 3
    COMPLEX LITIGATION 6
    GOVERNMENT INVESTIGATIONS 6

CHAPTER 2 – BECOMING A FORENSIC ACCOUNTANT 8
    MINIMUM REQUIREMENTS 8
    ESSENTIAL SKILLS 9
    BECOMING A FORENSIC ACCOUNTANT 10
    EARN YOUR DEGREE 10
    KEEP A GOOD CHARACTER 11
    MAKE YOURSELF KNOWN 11
    RESEARCH IS ESSENTIAL 11
    JOBS FOR FORENSIC ACCOUNTANTS 12

CHAPTER 3 – REASONS FORENSIC ACCOUNTANTS ARE INEFFECTIVE 16

CHAPTER 4 – MOST COMMON FRAUD SCHEMES 20
    SKIMMING 20
    WRITE-OFFS THAT ARE FRAUDULENT OR LAPPING 21
    USING SHELL COMPANIES 22

- Creating Ghost Employees 23
- Shrinkage of Inventory 24
- Management Embezzlement 25
- Security Fraud 25
- Uncovering the Truth 28

CHAPTER 5 – FORENSIC ACCOUNTING METHODS 29
- The Records 31
- Indirect and Direct Methods 32

CHAPTER 6 – FORENSIC ACCOUNTING FOR A DIVORCE 34
- How Forensic Accountants Help You 34
- Real Estate Fraud 35

CHAPTER 7 – HOW DOES A TRIAL WORK? 38
- Get Organized 38
- Organization as a Forensic Accountant 40

CHAPTER 8 – MINIMIZE THE RISK OF BUSINESS AND INDIVIDUALS 42

CHAPTER 9 – TECHNOLOGY AND TOOLS USED 46

CHAPTER 10 – LESSONS LEARNED 49
- The Enron Scandal 49
- The WorldCom Fraud 50
- The AIG Scandal 50
- Sir Paul McCartney and Heather Mills Divorce 51
- Al Capone's Tax Evasion 51
- Robert Maxwell's Embezzlement 52
- O.J. Simpson's Millions 52

CHAPTER 11 – THINGS TO REMEMBER 53
- The Seven Common Risks 56

CHAPTER 12: HOW INTERNSHIPS CAN HELP YOU BREAK INTO FORENSIC ACCOUNTING 59

CHAPTER 13: INTERNAL CONTROL POLICIES	65
CHAPTER 14: A FEW COMMON EXAMPLES OF GENERAL FRAUD	69
CHAPTER 15: AUDITING AND FORENSIC ACCOUNTING	73
CHAPTER 16: OBTAINING A FORENSIC ACCOUNTANT MASTERS DEGREE	77
CHAPTER 17: TOOLS FORENSIC ACCOUNTANTS MAY USE	81
CHAPTER 18: THE SKILLS A FORENSIC ACCOUNTANT NEEDS	84
CHAPTER 19: STUDYING FOR THE CPA	88
CHAPTER 20: PREPARING FOR TEST DAY	93
CHAPTER 21: A TYPICAL DAY-TO-DAY OF A FORENSIC ACCOUNTANT	95
CHAPTER 22: BECOMING A CERTIFIED FRAUD EXAMINER	97
CONCLUSION	100
CHECK OUT MORE BOOKS BY GREG SHIELDS	102

Introduction

What do Sherlock Holmes and forensic accounting have in common? The answer is simple: like Sherlock Holmes, forensic accounting is a detective. A *financial* detective.

This book will teach you how to become the 'Sherlock Holmes' of the accounting world. You will learn how financial officers, auditors, police officers and other detectives rely on forensic accountants.

One of the first questions to ask is, *Was there a financial crime?* Through research, if the answer turns out to be no, the case is closed. However, if the evidence suggests a potential financial crime, the real work begins.

You may wonder, *What type of person becomes a forensic accountant?* This book will detail not only what it takes to be one, but also how to be good at it. Moreover, it will give you insight into career prospects. Some people believe financial detectives are ineffective; however, you will learn why this is, and how, like any job, it has its ups and downs.

Throughout the following chapters, you will also learn about different types of fraud and how it is detected. Forensic accountants work largely with fraud cases. Thus, you will probably learn more about fraud in the subsequent pages than you did in school. Every business has financial statements and inventories, and you will learn how to review these statements and inventories through the eyes of a detective. Other areas of fraud, such as stocks, securities, and investments, will also be discussed.

Furthermore, you will learn how to trace money, obtain records, tap into the electronic evidence, and much more.

This book is centralized on one specific area; however, there is an entire chapter on minimizing the risk of your business or the individuals involved. You might have a brilliant detective on the case, but you can protect yourself to take minimum risks. Real-life examples of cases and situations will also be drawn upon to help you learn all the necessary and valuable lessons.

Knowledge is power, and once you have finished reading this book, you will be able to solve the financial mysteries of the world.

If you are ready to become a savvy, financial sleuth, let's get started!

Chapter 1 – What is Forensic Accounting?

Two areas encompass forensic accounting: Litigation Support and Investigation.

Litigation Support

This is a representation of issues that relate to issues in the economy, also known as 'litigation that is pending'. Often in court, damages have occurred and been sustained by both parties. It is the job of a forensic accountant to help resolve such disputes – preferably before the matter reaches the courtroom. However, if the dispute does go to court, a forensic accountant can testify. They are considered an expert witness, and because a typical accountant does not know their way around a courtroom, this sets a forensic accountant apart as they have courtroom knowledge to their advantage.

Investigation

A forensic accountant *investigates* the issues. Part of their job is to find out if there is some form of criminal activity, such as security or insurance fraud, or employee or identity theft. They may also be asked to help with civil matters and divorce cases. Fraud auditing and forensic accounting are similar. However, with fraud auditing there is some control over the situation to prevent it from happening; whereas with forensic accounting, one is hired to investigate after the situation has already happened. An example of a typical case is a company suspecting embezzlement, fraud or theft, and so they hire a forensic accountant to investigate.

A forensic accountant has thorough schooling and training in accounting. They must apply all their knowledge to issues relating to a legal aspect. Forensic accountants are asked to perform several duties, such as testifying in court, investigating fraud, help with criminal and civil investigations, and writing reports.

Financial abuse is everywhere, and a forensic accountant *must* be an expert. Their knowledge is a powerful tool for battling financial abuse and detecting fraud, so their role is vital and will continue to be in demand. They will be used more for prosecuting those who commit fraud and will also educate and prevent future fraud within a business.

One significant challenge a forensic accountant faces is a changing landscape. Due to technology, the online world is rapidly changing. There is now an overwhelming concern for keeping company files safe. This has opened a new door for committing fraud which is easier to hide. A company needs to ensure that their files are safe as most now store their information online.

A business may hire an accountant to do their books in-house. This is great, as they can continue to minimize and monitor the irregularities and complications which always come up within a business. However, there will still be instances involving fraudulent activity. A regular accountant is all about the numbers and making things balance. Thanks to technology, it is easier to make everything balance on the books and still hide the activities of fraud. Thus, an accountant may never detect it.

Over the years, the need for forensic accounting has continued to rise. Forensic accountants are proficient and experts in finance and accounting matters. However, their expertise doesn't stop there. As businesses begin to venture further into the digital age, there is a growing concern over crimes such as fraud within a company. Skills are needed to battle these issues with the online world, and such skills revolve around understanding computer technologies. Moreover, the legal process is critical in achieving an outcome in the event of an issue going to court.

A few chief factors have brought forensic accounting to where it is today. One of these factors is the new generation. Many new business professionals and entrepreneurs are coming onto the scene. For example, 500,000 new businesses start up every year. Out of these 500,000, most have a major aspect that is based online or, at least, a partial foothold on it.

As the broader business world changes, grows and becomes more reliant on the digital world, the career role for a forensic accountant expands. Even in the United States military where they have complex passwords, there is still a level of risk. A password must be around twelve to fifteen characters, with at least two uppercase and two lowercase letters, two numbers and two special characters. There might not seem to be a security risk with such a complex password, but the simple truth is that there is. Anything online is at risk. Because the digital world is a continually changing environment, the skills and various methods used for these investigations also changing. They *must* keep up with digital evolution.

At times, there are clues in emails, folders, forms, and files. Somewhere there is some form of communication that is talking about the fraud that is happening. That is why a forensic accountant searches through all these forms of communication.

In Sherlock Holmes' day, fraud was far easier to detect and find. However, looking back on some cases, aspects were not so easy. What is meant by this is that people had a harder time masking what was going on. After the Internet was created, more and more businesses and people flocked toward the digital age. This allowed for fraud to become sophisticated – almost to the point of devastating. Thus emerged the forensic accountant, a sought-after specialist with a significant role in civil litigation and criminal justice.

Based on the American Institute of CPAs (AICPA), there is anticipated growth in forensic accounting. There have been changes with the regulatory enforcement, and it is expected that a spur of positions within CPAs will be experts in forensics. *Why is the future so bright and clear for accounting in forensics?* Let's look at this in-depth:

Complex Litigation

Lawyers are highly knowledgeable in most legal matters. However, even they can need outside sources for additional information. When it comes to financial disputes, they also tend to call in experts. A forensic accountant can decipher some of the most complicated issues in the financial realm. They then pass such information on to clients and attorneys in understandable English. There are also times when an investigative role will need to be played in civil cases. This is where the forensic accountant will work together with attorneys to investigate any assets or income that has not been reported.

Government Investigations

Forensic accountants are extremely useful within large government investigations. They can track the most complex of money trails, and some consultants who are not agents are employed at a state or regional level. However, regarding sensitive matters, these are usually handled by forensic accountants employed by the FBI. The FBI employees hundreds of these accountants due to the nature of their investigative abilities. There are five main entry programs for special agents of the FBI; accounting qualifies as one of those programs. Other major employers for the government are the SEC's Enforcement Division and the IRS.

Risk Management and Prevention

There are agencies at both the corporate and government level who are looking more toward experts in forensic accounting. Forensic accountants aid with prevention measures designed to keep fraud associated with expenses of an investigation or litigation processes at a minimum. An internal audit is one among many things a forensic accountant might be asked to perform. These audits are used to find any potential pitfalls. Once the problem areas have been identified, the accountant can assist nonprofit and corporate clients to begin the steps needed to minimize any potential fraud. In the corporate world, these accountants will monitor the emerging regulations and ensure the corporation complies.

Chapter 2 – Becoming a Forensic Accountant

The future is in high demand for forensic accountants. So much so that this avenue of law enforcement is the fastest-growing field.

In such a digital world, these super financial detectives are on the case. They search for clues to solve the case. When there is money involved, so is a forensic accountant. Here are some areas where a forensic accountant might be required:

> ➤ Performing forensic audits.

> ➤ Following the clues and evidence to identify any discrepancies in the funds for both public and private companies, including the government.

> ➤ Preparing an expert witness testimony for both civil and criminal cases.

> ➤ Reviewing statements from the fortune 500 companies, and smaller firms.

Minimum Requirements

Each state is slightly different regarding the requirements to become a forensic accountant. To become certified, you follow much of the same requirements for becoming a traditional accountant. You need a Bachelor of Accounting or a bachelor in a related subject. You will also be required to sit national exams and follow state requirements as you obtain your Certified Public Accountant (CPA) license. Most states necessitate all candidates to complete 150 hours of coursework at college. This is about thirty hours more than the usual four-year bachelor's degree.

For a position in forensic accounting, you must have a minimum of one to three years of experience in accounting. If you are working as a general accountant, then you have already met this requirement.

There are times where an employer may require or encourage you to peruse the Certified Fraud Examiner credentials. These credentials give you the knowledge to perform investigations. Remember, forensic accountants are the experts. With these credentials, you will have a clear understanding of the fraud and analysis of data procedures. This advanced understanding shall assist in searching for any criminal activity.

The Bureau of Labor Statistics stated that they expect jobs in accounting to rise 13% by 2020. Thus, as crimes in America and throughout the world increase, there will be a larger demand for forensic accountants.

Essential Skills

Several skills are essential for becoming a forensic accountant. It is a given that you must have substantial knowledge of legal matters and be highly proficient at accounting. However, you must have other factors as well:

> ➤ A remarkable curiosity for wanting to know the truth.

> ➤ The little details are important. You must pay attention to every little detail to find the clues.

> ➤ Do not take the easy solution. Be persistent to find the answers you need.

> ➤ A creative mind goes a long way. Sometimes the answer is not right in front of you. You may need to get creative to find all the clues.

> Communication is key. There will be times you will need to testify professionally or write up reports. It is hugely important to know how to communicate all your findings effectively.

> As you do your research and investigations you will find that having great knowledge and an ability to perform analytics and research will be essential.

With all this talk about being a forensic accountant, you should ask yourself, *Is this a good job for me?* To be honest, only you can answer this life-changing yet straightforward question. Keep in mind that, generally, you need a Bachelor of Forensic Science, Biology, Chemistry, or Accounting. The annual median salary is ~$56,320.

Becoming a Forensic Accountant

So, what does it take to be a forensic accountant? Here are four fundamental steps:

1. Undertake a program to get your degree or obtain experience in a related field.

2. Become a Certified Public Accountant and pass the examination.

3. Apply for forensic accountant jobs.

4. Get hired.

Those are the basic steps to getting a job as a forensic accountant. However, there is more to the process, so let's expand on these steps:

Earn Your Degree

Like most careers, you need a university degree. So the first step is to find an accredited college and get a formal education. Detectives are great at solving mysteries, but you do not need to be one for you to know how important your education is. To be the best in this field, you will want to become a Certified Public Accountant. Rules and laws are always changing, so even if you have all these credentials, you are still always learning. We all want to succeed, and you may want to seek further education and receive your Certified Fraud Examiner certification.

Keep A Good Character

Good character is very important. You are interested in forensic accounting and thus have a great appreciation for justice. This is a great start. Having a good, moral character and this appreciation will be an essential part of the position of a forensic accountant. You will be asked to testify as a professional and must be trustworthy and honest in all situations. There is an extensive background check, which means that even before you decide to become a forensic accountant, you need to have a spotless record.

Make Yourself Known

Being known to the accounting and legal world does not happen overnight. It happens over time through gaining experience. A great way to gain experience is while you are going to school. Take the time to show you have a desire to work with risk management, risk reduction, and auditing. Do not get discouraged if there is not a forensic accountant job opening at that time. Try gaining experience through accounting via the government. Some tasks will overlap with forensic accounting and will help you gain experience. This will also ensure a great referral when an opening becomes available.

Research is Essential

Research is an important part of landing the perfect job in forensic accounting. The work that is done will retrieve and prevent trillions of lost dollars due to foul play. This is one reason why it is one of the fastest growing careers in the accounting industry.

Some of the areas you want to research are job outlook, salary and where you can work:

➢ **Job Outlook:** The accounting field is steadily growing, and a little faster than the average rate. By 2020, there is an expected 13% increase in jobs. This is just accounting in general, so forensic accountants will be in even higher demand.

➢ **Salary:** The annual median salary of an accountant is ~$63,550. However, because there is such a high demand for forensic accountants, their median is set at ~$74,000 annually. Keep in mind that location is everything. Depending on the location, there is potential to earn a six-figure salary. For example, a forensic accountant in Idaho may only earn $74,000, while in New York City, where crime is higher, they could earn $100,000 annually.

➢ **Where you can work:** You can be employed both with the private and public sector. In the private sector, you could work for a company lowering or reducing risks of potential internal fraud. You could also work for a company to investigate assets for the means of a fair divorce settlement. A forensic accountant can be used in all areas of investigations. *What about a federal agency?* Yes, even on the federal side there are jobs for. You might be hired to help with law enforcement agencies like the Secret Service, NCIS and FBI, with the sole purpose of uncovering and revealing the truth.

Jobs for Forensic Accountants

What types of jobs are out there for a forensic accountant? And what types of agencies need to hire one? Here is a list of the responsibilities of each potential agency. Keep in mind that all of these requires both experience and education:

Government agencies and departments

The government is always a huge target. These agencies include the IRS, CIA, and FBI. A forensic accountant's duties may include:

- Being asked to investigate the financial history of criminals, spies, and terrorists.

- Testifying in court as an expert witness.

- Building a financial profile on any suspicious suspects or individuals.

- Gathering any evidence and help in executing search warrants.

- Participating in interrogations.

- Tracking down illicit sources of funding.

- Compiling financial investigative reports.

- Meeting with prosecutors to discuss their strategies.

Accounting firms

You may be surprised that an accounting firm needs a forensic accountant working for them. A forensic accountant's duties may include:

- Uncovering fraud that could be happening and collect evidence.

- Translating technical jargon so those who do not understand the technical side can understand it through everyday language.

- Going to court and testifying.

- Conducting computer forensics.

- Having a fact-finding type of interview.

- Quantifying the financial losses that are due because of misconduct.

The Corporate Security & Risk Management areas

Corporate Securities and Risk Management are two big areas that are in need of a forensic accountant. A forensic accountant's duties may include:

> ➤ Protecting the financial assets from external and internal threats. This will also include any economic circumstances and political issues.

> ➤ Analyzing changes in exchange rates, taxes, and the cultural attitude to include their influences on the profits and operations.

> ➤ Ensuring that the organization follows all procedures and laws.

> ➤ Auditing all financial statements and looking for risks.

Law Firms

Forensic accountants regularly work with the law, and it is only natural that law firms will have a demand for them. A forensic accountant's duties may include:

> ➤ Law firms don't know much about financial issues so you would act as a consultant within the firm.

> ➤ In a law firm, financial information is like a foreign language. You will need to translate the more complex finding into a language they can understand.

> ➤ You will be required to assist with the findings as a financial expert and to give testimony as such.

> ➤ Audits are always a big issue, and you will be performing these audits for all investigations.

Financial Consulting Firms

You would think these firms would have experts in all financial matters. However, most of the time, they only have accountants who specialize in their individual areas of expertise. A forensic account is an expert in all areas and can assist in investigations via the firm. Their duties may include:

> ➢ Investigating corruption, regulatory scrutiny, and fraud.
>
> ➢ Reconstructing and analyzing digital information and financial records.
>
> ➢ Performing interviews to get information.
>
> ➢ Assessing the vulnerability for fraud.
>
> ➢ Investigating any allegations of embezzlement.

These are only a few examples of forensic accountant jobs. You may also consider jobs in management accounting, public accounting, financial accounting, auditing and government accounting. Such jobs do not always pertain to forensics; however, they will give you the necessary experience to pursue a job as a forensic accountant.

Chapter 3 – Reasons Forensic Accountants are Ineffective

Despite the critical roles expert forensic accountants play, they can be less effective in two specific areas – as attorneys and CPAs.

The following details nine reasons why forensic accountants can be ineffective as attorneys and CPAs, and how these areas rank against one another. Keep in mind that we are talking about forensic accountants in both types of fields.

Inability to simplify information

It is important to be able to present the required information in a simple and easy to understand way. Attorneys are not good at simplifying information. In fact, they ranked #1 with about 89% of attorneys not being able to simplify their findings. Anyone who has been in a courtroom will know why this is #1 among lawyers. However, a CPA ranked #4 with 66%. As you can see, both areas have a strong issue with the ability to simplify information.

Ineffective oral communication

Being able to speak and communicate orally is a valuable skill in any job. It is especially important for a forensic accountant. Attorneys ranked at #2 as the most ineffective, with 80% not knowing how to communicate, while CPAs ranked #3 with 68% not knowing how to communicate effectively. Again, both ranked in the top five for the nine reasons. *Why is communication such a huge problem?* As a forensic accountant, it is vital to communicate effectively.

Inability to understand the goals of a case

Understanding is another area that is very important in forensic accounting. *Why is it so hard to understand the issues and details of a case?* Strangely, attorneys made the top five with 67% ranking them at #3. CPAs tend to have a marginally better understanding which did not put them in the top five; however, it still was quite high at 55%.

Inability to identify key issues

Finding the key issues in any case is imperative. Attorneys are supposed to be good at this, yet they ranked #4 in the top five with 65% struggling in this area, whereas CPAs ranked #1 at 72%.

Lack of investigative intuitiveness

Detectives would be good in this area. Attorneys are supposed to be good with investigations but still ranked #5 with 57%, while CPAs ranked #2 with 68%.

Ineffective written communication

Written communication is just as important as oral. Both attorneys and CPAs did better in this area. However, CPAs still ranked in the top five at #5 with 64%, while attorneys did not rank in the top five – at 40%. It seems like one of the key factors of communication is also one of the strongest weaknesses.

Inability to synthesize

One thing that both groups did better was combining all the details and facts to see the bigger picture. The numbers are still high, but not high enough for them to be in the top five. Attorneys had 56%, and CPAs had 49%. What is interesting is how CPAs do slightly better in this area.

Inflexible/close-minded

Often, attorneys and CPAs have their minds already set on the answer and are determined to find evidence to support it. They will reject facts that oppose their theories and accept facts that support them. Even though neither group is in the top five, they are both high in percentages. Attorneys have 47%, while CPA's have 59%. Therefore, attorneys appear to be slightly more open-minded than CPAs.

It is a little hard to understand the rankings of why attorneys and CPAs are so ineffective. So let's look at the following chart. Each group is organized in order of their ineffectiveness:

Inevectiveness of Attorneys as a Forensic Accountant		
ISSUE	%	Rank
Inability to simplify the information	89%	1
Ineffective oral communication	80%	2
Inability to understand the goals of a case	67%	3
Inability to identify key issues	65%	4
Lack of investigative intuitiveness	57%	5
Inability to synthesize	56%	6
Not flexable / close-minded	47%	7
Ineffective written communication	40%	8
Other	3%	9

Inevectiveness of CPA's as a Forensic Accountant		
ISSUE	%	Rank
Inability to identify key issues	72%	1
Lack of investigative intuitiveness	68%	2
Ineffective oral communication	68%	3
Inability to simplify the information	66%	4
Ineffective written communication	64%	5
Not flexible / close-minded	59%	6
Inability to understand the goals of a case	55%	7
Inability to synthesize	49%	8
Other	4%	9

Looking at these numbers, you can see where the concern is with forensic accountants. Each of these areas is critical to being a detective. The problem is that there are so many who fail in such areas. There are only a handful of attorneys and CPAs that do not fall within these percentages. With the numbers being so high, that means that only a handful of forensic accountants have what it takes to be effective at the job.

Resources:

AICPA. (n.d.). *Characteristics and Skills of the Forensic Accountant.* Retrieved from the AICPA website: https://www.aicpa.org/InterestAreas/ForensicAndValuation/Resources/PractAidsGuidance/DownloadableDocuments/ForensicAccountingResearchWhitePaper.pdf

Chapter 4 – Most Common Fraud Schemes

One of the most challenging aspects is the millions of fraud cases that out there. The following chapter details the most common schemes. This is a good place to start as most cases begin or end with one of these.

Skimming

When a company or organization has cash transactions, then they are vulnerable to skimming from employees. Skimming is when an employee asks for slightly more than what the business is asking – for a product or service – and pockets the extra. Alternatively, another example would be charging the customer the asking price and then recording it as a discount and pocketing the difference.

Skimming is common with professional practices which accept fees paid in cash. For example, a cashier who takes in cash and does not record it in the accounting record. Or maybe they did, but the transaction was deliberately deleted.

Medical practices can also be vulnerable to such fraud. This is due to how small cash copayments are. Most of the time, the patient is not concerned about a receipt. After all, with small copayments, there is no refund they could receive.

With this being one of the most common types of fraud, what can a business or organization do to protect itself? This is where management gets together and looks into their policies in-depth. A great way is to include in the policy that it is mandatory to give a receipt to the customer for all transactions, regardless if they want it or not. There should also be a copy of the receipt included in the files of the customer and the company. All three receipts must match. This way, when there is an audit, multiple sources show the amount. For added security, surveillance equipment can be placed in areas where cash is accepted – you often see this at banks.

Retailers can further be subject to skimming as they sell their products or merchandise through the exchange of cash. One way this can happen is from an employee keeping the store open after hours and pocketing the profits, as they do not have the additional financial details logged in the accounting record.

Skimming also still occurs within merchandising companies; however, as they are working with sales that have an exchange of goods, skimming leads to inventory shrinkage. Inventory shrinkage is discussed later in this chapter as it is also one of the most common fraud schemes.

Write-Offs that are Fraudulent or Lapping

As we examined, skimming tends to deal with cash transactions. *But what if a customer pays with a check or another form of payment?* For example, write-offs or lapping can be made by mailroom employees. Perhaps they are the ones who will take in the payments? If so, that means that they can skim on the checks they receive. *So how do they do it?*

The employee takes the payment, and instead of putting it into the company's account, they deposit the check into their personal account. When there is no cover-up, the scheme is foiled quickly – the company will send a second notice or bill to the customer stating that the bill is overdue. Thus, the company finds out there is an issue when the customer provides a copy of the canceled check. However, things are not always that easy. This type of fraud can be covered up by fraudulent write-offs and lapping.

Let's discuss how a cover-up works and take the example of someone in a company stealing a payment made by Mr. Jones. When Mr. Alex pays his bill, it is applied to Mr. Jones' account. Eventually, when Mr. Smith pays his bill, it is allied to account of Mr. Alex. This cycle will continue and hide the fact that there is a missing payment.

Another solid cover-up is to write-off the bill. As we discussed, if the bill has not been paid, then a second bill is sent out, which means that the employee who stole the check needs to make sure that the second bill never gets sent. Thus, they write it off the books.

A positive thing nowadays is online payments which, in turn, start to eliminate the threat of skimming. However, if a company still takes in cash or checks, then it must look into some internal security measures to protect its business.

Using Shell Companies

Higher management or employees typically create shell companies. These companies sell fictitious services and goods. The bill goes out for these services and goods, and the person who owns the shell company will sign off on the disbursement to the company they work for. As these payments are made, the individual who owns the shell company has now stolen money from the parent company.

Usually, a P.O. Box or residential address is used as the business address. Due to the fraudulent employee's address being on file with the parent company, the employee may use a spouse or a relative's address to set up the shell company. Shell company bills, however, are missing one key element – authenticity. For example, a secretary of a company starts to notice something irregular on the bills. Each bill has the company's address, but it is the same address as a supervisor at the company.

Another example is when bills from the shell company have invoices that are all in order. This is a red flag. *Why are they all in order? Do they not have any other customers?* In fact, the organization is the only vendor. Thus, this starts an investigation into the shell company and reveals the fictitious vendor and the fraud.

An interesting thing to note is that shell companies do not always sell fictitious services and goods. *But if they sell legitimate goods, then how is it a shell company?* The answer is that the price is just inflated. Drop shipping is an example of this. Granted, this is legal. However, when higher-level employees of the company do it, and they sell to the company, it is not as legal as you may think. With drop shipping, a product is taken from another source and shipped directly to the customer by that company. A higher rate is charged to make a profit. With a shell company, it is similar; however, it is directed to the parent company that the fraudulent employees work for, with the purpose to steal from the parent company.

Any time you are working for a company, it is important to check their list of vendors and get verification.

Creating Ghost Employees

Ghost employees is a fraudulent scheme common among managers of Human Resources and Payroll. These two areas are in the position to create and delete employees who do not "actually" work for the company. These employees are then added to the payroll and personnel records and thus get a "monthly paycheck". For this reason, ghost employees are dangerous for companies as they cost them vast amounts of money.

Unfortunately, this type of fraud is the hardest to detect. Once a ghost employee is created, it looks like any other employee account-wise. The fraudulent employee who is collecting the stolen money does not need to maintain the ghost employee's account or do anything else, except when it comes to payday. Whenever a new employee is created, they must be listed in all the databases of the company. Human Resources and Payroll only have access to a select few, which means that detecting this fraud scheme requires employee data to be compared with all the databases of the company. If there is still fraud, but it shows up in multiple databases, then several employees might be working together to share the illegal profits. Some areas to check are days off, vacation days, work performance, etc., as ghost employees do not "actually" work for the company. Thus, all these areas will show no data.

Shrinkage of Inventory

We earlier discussed skimming. *However, what if it's not money being stolen, and inventory instead?* When a business sells products, there is usually a sales and inventory account that is affected. Granted, when a person steals the inventory, the sale isn't recorded, and thus there is a decrease in inventory. So now, there is inventory that is unaccounted for in the balance. Whenever a business has inventory, they will have some shrinkage due to normal business operations. It is the unusual shrinkage that causes the concerns and red flags.

Any time there is a normal shrinkage or an event causes it, all items within the business' inventory are affected. When this happens, there is no trend or pattern for the inventory shrinkage. When there *is* a trend or pattern, then an investigation may show a fraud scheme.

For several organizations, recording a shrinkage in inventory can be difficult. These are the two most common methods:

> ➤ **Periodic System:** With this system, the balance of the inventory is computed or estimated at intervals that are periodic.

> ➤ **Perpetual System:** With this system, sales of inventory and all transfer-in inventory are recorded.

A business tends to only use one system to reduce the risk of the inventory being off. *So how can a shrinkage be detected?* With a perpetual system, the system must be implemented to keep a running total of all the inventory, which can be verified through physical observation. When there are discrepancies between the two amounts or balances, then it will show the amount of shrinkage in inventory.

For this shrinkage to be hidden, there needs to be either a change in the perpetual records of inventory or management of the actual count of inventory. Therefore, it is vital to have a segregation of duties and some internal control procedures. This will make it harder to conceal the inventory being stolen.

Management Embezzlement

This can happen in any organization – small or large, corporate or military.

Let's look at the example of Tyco International. They had three senior officers who were charged for the embezzlement of millions of dollars. One of these officers was the CEO of the company. Due to their status within the company, they could exonerate loans to each other – thus they were stealing from the company. When caught, they were charged for the theft of >$170,000,000 of company loans.

Another example is within the military. A Sergeant First Class worked in Finance for the United States Army. He oversaw the collection of funds from vendors and other soldiers. He would transfer only a few cents or dollars of each transaction into his bank account. It was a very small amount, which meant that it was extremely hard to detect. *So how did he get caught*? Well, his fellow soldiers reported it, and an investigation was started. He was charged for stealing >$10,000 or government funds.

Security Fraud

You have probably noticed the tighter restrictions with banks. This was caused by the series of financial collapses that occurred after the global recession. Security fraud is a serious crime. Typically, it is committed by an entire brokerage firm or an individual. They used to hold back information from the investors for the purpose to manipulate the performance of the stock market. By not giving investors all of the information, it can convince them to invest more in a company that may appear to be strong on paper but really isn't. These investors could lose a lot of money based on this incorrect information. One way to combat such fraud is to hire a forensic accountant. They will thoroughly look through the financial statements for clues that will support any claims of fraud.

Based on the information that is in the SEC filings, and any other documents the investor will use, a company to go into litigation. When this occurs, a forensic accountant will investigate to see if there is evidence of security fraud. There are several ways security fraud can occur:

Misrepresentation of information in the SEC filing

Companies who are publicly traded file SEC reports. An investor will typically use these reports to help determine if this company will be a good investment. If this information is filed with misleading information about the company's performance and assets, a crime has been committed. In turn, this could lead to civil charges and litigation of the company.

An investigation happens when there is a suspicion of security fraud. One thing that is looked at in-depth is the financial statements. If there is any security fraud, it is possible that there will be a history of it somewhere within the records of the business.

Performing account fraud

After the recession, the Dodd-Frank Wall Street Reform and Consumer Protection Act was introduced. Within the act, there are disclosure requirements that all corporations are must adhere to. This act was created to reform the financial regulations and increase the transparency. What is discouraging is how companies fail at a venture or have taken an investment risk that didn't pay off, and then try to hide the debts and losses.

A forensic accountant has vast knowledge about what the security regulations and the Generally Accepted Accounting Principles require. With this knowledge, they can go through a company's records and find the hidden losses to decide if the firm was giving investors misleading information.

Engaging a form of insider trading

Let's say someone worked for a big corporation and they had valuable information. This information could affect the value of the company's stock or assets. This would be a great temptation to use to invest in the company, such as insider trading. *What if they knew the company was seeing the dangers of bankruptcy?* They knew this would greatly affect the stock of the company once the news was released. Taking their stocks, they begin to sell them while they are still high and thus make a substantial profit. They could take this even further and try to sell this information to investors of the company.

Insider trading is a big issue among investors and company employees. When an employee is dealing with the accusations of security fraud, their reputation is destroyed. The personal accounts and the reconstructed transactions are the places to look for this fraud.

Putting money toward a scam or another form of hedge fund

You hear about a company misappropriating a fund and wonder why they would do this. However, this is another way to defraud investors. Using the money that is for investors and misappropriating a fund is fraud. This is where hedge funds come in. Stolen money from a parent fund is deposited into these "hedge funds" instead. This means that the investor gave money and expected a specific return, but instead, the money was used for something else.

Most of the time, investors do not realize that their investment is part of a Ponzi and Pyramid scheme. When a forensic accountant investigates these schemes, they follow the money trail to the end.

Uncovering the Truth

Uncovering the truth with these scams and schemes is the job of a forensic accountant. They will use their skills and knowledge to dig into the financial records of a company to seek out potential fraud.

These security frauds will also cover investment and stock fraud. The sole purpose is to seduce the investors into making financial decisions that are based on the false information that has been reported.

Chapter 5 – Forensic Accounting Methods

Forensic accounting is about investigating the clues and following the trail. Several areas are examined, and most times, one needs to follow the money trail. Sometimes this is as easy as checking bank records or as hard as needing to investigate one back to another, as the money is floated until it reaches its final destination.

Tracing money is a tedious job and can take days or months to find the source and crack the case. For a simple case, the individual has a little bit wired to a specific account which will be their account or someone they know. This is an example like the Sargent First Class from the previous chapter.

Another example is an employee that is wiring money from the company's funds to their personal account. However, it is not a direct wire. Instead, they wire to a dummy account. It will stay in this dummy account for a couple of days, then is electronically transferred to another account which is also a dummy account. It could easily follow this pattern for months before it ever gets to the intended account for the employee who stole the money. Keep in mind that even this account may be a dummy, and they can access it through other means.

It is a great challenge to find money and catch up to it as the money is floated from one bank to another. On top of that, the employee may have access to each of these accounts to drain the funds slowly. For example, $10,000 that was stolen might only be $500 by the time it reaches the end bank. By the time the investigation catches up to the money, the employee already has $9,500 that has been deposited into their real account by using very small amounts. This makes it harder to detect and will not raise red flags with their bank.

When a forensic accountant locks onto the money trail and starts to see all the banks it has gone through, they then investigate each of those accounts and find out that a small amount has been withdrawn each time. *Did the fraudulent employee use a card and withdraw the money? If so, was it withdrawn in the same location each time? Was it in the same city or state?* When the employee uses an ATM card, it is recorded. If they are going from state to state to make the withdrawals, then the accountant needs to anticipate or find out where the next bank is and where the employee may access the money. This is where things get tricky. Thus, you can see why a forensic accountant must be the *best* when it comes to both accounting and investigating.

Another part of all investigations is obtaining records. Several years ago, records used to be all hard copies. They were not kept electronically. That means more paperwork and a longer process to request the records to be sent by the company. Clues will come from company records. A forensic accountant wants to know the employees and staff so well that people would think they are the boss or CEO. They will start asking questions like, *What type of person is each individual?* And *What is the situation in their life?* These are basic questions that will give the accountant a list of people to start considering.

Today, most records are electronic and easier to request. It does not take as long to get the records, and the investigation will not stop because of the records. With all this information, a forensic accountant needs to be organized. It is crucial for them to know their way around programs like Word, Excel, and Access.

The Records

When there is a document that will provide a bigger outlook on an investigation, then it is a record of interest. That means a forensic accountant will have memos, e-mails, databases, ledgers, journals, credit statements, bank statements, etc.

Once they have all the records in order and have examined the information, it is time for interviews. Now the investigation can move forward. These interviews are not only with the employees the records indicate to, but also with anyone who knows information about the case. If someone has access to the records, they need to be interviewed. If they noticed the irregularities, they need to be interviewed. A forensic accountant is a detective and thus must suspect everyone.

As the interviews are conducted, the interviewees' behaviors are observed for clues. They are not going to tell the truth – even though that would make the case easier to solve – so the accountant must look for clues of them taking several vacations or purchasing things like a new car. For example, if an employee is only on a minimum wage and has a family of five, the odds are that they cannot afford to go on several vacations or a brand-new car. Granted, this alone does not say made them fraudulent, so further examination of their finances is needed. Maybe they have another job and source of income? All of this information helps build the bigger picture.

The context of the case will depend on how far a forensic accountant needs to look for information. When the case is of a criminal nature, then they work with the district attorney's office and law enforcement.

But how does one obtain such records to begin with? The answer is that the companies or individuals give them to you. This is where the relationship with the district attorney's office and law enforcement come in handy. In situations that require it, a search warrant or subpoena must be obtained. It is also important to know that companies and banks have client and employee confidentiality agreements. This means that even if there is a criminal investigation, they cannot give this information to anyone except the client or employee – unless there is a signed document by them stating otherwise.

Now that a forensic accountant has the records and interviews gathered, their notes are organized, and it is time to start their analysis of the findings. This may require a trace of all the assets the company has. Then the accountant will need to calculate the total losses, document how the theft occurred, and summarize the various transactions involved. Once the analysis is complete, it is time to write up the report. The report must be thorough and include spreadsheets, charts, and graphs. A good rule of thumb is to add an in-depth summary of findings and include all organized notes in the report as supporting evidence. This will incorporate all records of information found. Unless the forensic accountant is asked to testify in court, this report is their last step in the investigation.

Indirect and Direct Methods

Through the direct method, an examiner will look at all the public notices, records, agreements, contracts, invoices, and canceled checks. There may also be interviews with the employees and management.

The indirect method will include the bank deposit method and the net worth method.

The Net Worth Method

This method calculates the company or individual's total assets and then subtracts the total liabilities. The result of this calculation is the net worth. That net worth is then compared over many periods. An investigation may go in several directions depending on if there are unreconciled differences.

The Bank Deposit Method

Through this method, total deposits made during the year are analyzed and then compared with the total expenses. If there are any transfers between accounts, they are subtracted from the total deposits for that year to arrive at the net deposits. The total expenditures for that year will be added to the net deposits to give a total receipt for the year. This number will be compared to the funds from any known sources which will determine the total amount of funds from the unknown sources. The forensic accountant will now start to investigate the unknown sources. This investigation may include searching or tracking information for the specific amount in question. It may also require them to interview key individuals as they come up in the investigation.

All these methods are essential to an investigation and will bring the detective closer to finding the truth.

Chapter 6 – Forensic Accounting for a Divorce

When divorces get complicated, or a spouse does not trust the other and thinks there is information or assets that are being hidden, or things like child support and alimony are complex to figure out, a forensic accountant can help to ensure that there are no issues with the paperwork and filings. For example, they can find and uncover any hidden assets or streams of income and trace any liabilities and assets each party may have.

How Forensic Accountants Help You

Every divorce is different. That means the information in this chapter is only basic knowledge. It is important to note that a forensic accountant is *not* a lawyer. They can only uncover information and help with the financial side of things. Granted, they can work with a lawyer to find the information for someone.

While the lawyer is working on the divorce case, a forensic accountant is working on the financial documents. They are interested in all the documents that pertain to any information that will reveal the financials of a spouse – both business and personal. These documents may include mortgage applications, business projects, appointment books, credit card statements, bank statements, and tax returns. This is only a small list of the documents that a forensic accountant will be looking to obtain. Keep in mind that they will need any document that shows a financial aspect.

A forensic accountant may utilize a financial account in various ways:

They can search for hidden income and assets

One would like to think that a spouse is entirely open about their finances. However, this is a divorce situation, which means that there might be something hidden, like a bank account or property. This is when the clues throughout bank statements and other records are essential.

They can search for inconsistencies

A forensic accountant knows what to look for. They examine the financial documents and all other documents of importance for anything that may look as if it is being hidden.

They can corroborate financial information

With a set skill in investigating, they can research and ensure that the financial information is in line with the non-financial information.

They can provide a valuation of a business

Most of the time a spouse does not know the actual value of an existing business. A forensic accountant can find and perform this valuation.

They can figure out the cash flow

A forensic accountant can calculate the support payments.

These are only a few areas. A forensic accountant can perform in several other aspects.

Real Estate Fraud

This is a huge issue among divorcees. Sometimes, a spouse is involved in real estate without the other spouse knowing.

What is real estate fraud and how does it pertain to divorces? Let's look at this example: a house will have its assets split between two parties. One party knows more about real estate than the other party. This means that they could lie about how much the real estate is worth or any information about the assets. The purpose is for them to get a bigger share as the lawyer and judge do not know the actual value.

There are a few fraud schemes in real estate that a forensic accountant may look for:

Mortgage Fraud

This fraud might involve a controlling spouse who has taken out a mortgage and withheld correct information from the other spouse. They did this to get a better rate, and thus misrepresented or possibly omitted crucial data relating to the real estate. This will result in several transactions that are fraudulent.

Foreclosure Fraud

This fraud might involve a controlling spouse that has real estate foreclosed on wrongly. At least, it appears that way. This leads the other spouse to think that they don't own the house. When the divorce takes place, because the innocent spouse believes that the house is not theirs, they move out due to the separation, while the controlling spouse still lives there or temporarily moves out for "show".

Title Fraud

This fraud might involve a title that has both spouse names on it. Suddenly, the title is fraudulently changed so that it only has one spouse on it. This means the property is individually owned instead of joint, and the other spouse may not have the right to a portion of the real estate.

Value Fraud

This fraud might involve spouses who cannot decide who gets the house, and the assets of the real estate will be divided through the value of what it is worth. This fraud happens when that value is deliberately misreported. This means that the assets will be split based on the false information and the controlling party may bank on the extra worth of the property.

Chapter 7 – How Does a Trial Work?

Up to this point, a forensic accountant could have already spent hours, days or weeks on the investigation. Having all their information organized for trial is essential Otherwise, the judge may not allow it to be presented in the trial. This could also be the difference between a conviction and no conviction.

Keep in mind that going to trial is the job of a lawyer. A forensic accountant's job is to gather financial evidence, give that evidence to the lawyer, and testify in the trial as a professional examiner – if needed. Let's go over some necessary information about the trial process and how it ties in with the forensic accountant's job.

Get Organized

One of the most significant skills a lawyer and forensic accountant has is organization. Lawyers have a lot to remember and organize, and a great way to aid with this is a three-ring binder and numbered tabs. Each tab represents a new section. They also want a table of contents so the judge and parties can easily follow the contents. At a minimum, three identical copies are needed. The judge, prosecuting lawyer, and depending lawyer will all need this binder. Each lawyer will have additional notes in their individual binders to help remind them what needs to be presented or asked regarding the witnesses.

Let's look at each area that will be outlined by the lawyer, and see how a forensic accountant and their evidence plays a role in this part of the preparation for a trial. Not all these sections are mandatory, as each case is different. However, this is a basic layout:

Section one may be testimonial evidence

This section is straightforward. It is a list of witnesses that may be called to the stand to testify. These people have some knowledge of the situation:

> ➤ **The accused** might be asked to share their side of the story and possibly defend themselves. Remember, they are on trial, and their goal is to be acquitted.
>
> ➤ **People with records** that are relevant to the case. This could be people whom the forensic accountant had received information from for the report that was submitted.
>
> ➤ Experts such as a **forensic accountant** who will testify of the validity of the information within the reports presented. A forensic accountant is not the only type of expert that may be called. All experts will be listed.
>
> ➤ **Anyone who has knowledge** of what the accused was doing. This information could be crucial as it is coming from key witnesses.
>
> ➤ Friends and Family may be called to the stand to testify for the character of the accused. These **character witnesses** may be very helpful for the accused.

Even this section should be organized. Most judges like it in the order of who is called to testify. Most of the time each witness will need to be present at the trial. It is the job of the lawyer to ensure they know when and where the trial will be held. The lawyer will also prepare each witness by going through a series of questions that may be asked during the trial. However, this does not ensure the witness will be present. If it is a key witness, then a subpoena may be requested to demand that the witness is at the trial. Often, this will also require the witness to bring and provide evidence.

Section two may be documentary evidence

This section is the biggest part of what is being presented. This is where all the evidence will be presented in the form of exhibits. It must be organized, in order, and needs to be given to each party as a copy. *So what information must be listed in this section?* At a minimum, the lawyer must provide where it originated from, the person who produced the exhibit, why it is important, and the reason they have it. They also need to show that it was obtained in a legal way, such as via a search warrant.

Each court may have different requirements; however, if a forensic accountant obtained the information, it will be in this section. All the evidence that was uncovered throughout the investigation will further be listed here.

Forensic accountants mainly work with financials. This means that there will be a lot of evidence that could have personal information on them, such as a social security number or account number. This information needs to be marked out for security purposes.

Requirement to show authentication

This section could be pictures of the crime or even the written report by the forensic accountant showing that all the exhibits gathered are authentic and were obtained through the proper means.

These three parts are the minimum of what is needed to present a case. They highlight the start of getting organized and ready for a trial. A forensic accountant may play a part in each section. There are other areas that a lawyer will need to go through in preparation for trial, such as getting the exhibits presented in the trial as evidence.

Organization as a Forensic Accountant

When a forensic accountant is involved with a case, most of the evidence will come from them. That means they must be organized. The easiest way is to use an Excel spreadsheet and set up columns that show the required information a lawyer will need in their binder for each exhibit. The forensic accountant will also want a binder with all their evidence organized. This makes it easier for the lawyer to see what they want to use and organize the evidence in their trial binder.

A binder will look different from the one a lawyer provides. It might have the following categories listed:

> **Company Employee Records:** This is an employee's company file. A warrant or subpoena may be needed to obtain this information. If it was obtained through the individual or the company, the accountant needs to include how it was authorized and the proof that it was done so legally.

> **Bank Statements:** When a case requires bank statements, these need to be included in this section, along with how the information was obtained. If it was obtained through the bank, a legal document authorizing the forensic accountant to obtain this information must be included in this section.

> **Business Financial Statements:** If a business is involved then their financial statements are needed. This will also include the means of obtaining those statements.

> **Report:** This is a thorough summary of all findings that have been generated by a forensic accountant. Part of this report will include spreadsheets, graphs, pictures, etc. Keep in mind that the entire binder will be associated with the report and a copy given to the lawyer.

This is only a starting point. Considering that each case is different, a binder and notes may have different headings and information.

We have gone over the basics of how a forensic accountant gets organized and presents information to a lawyer. The lawyer then takes that information and prepares it for trial.

Chapter 8 – Minimize the Risk of Business and Individuals

We discussed fraud and investigations in length. However, a question remains, *How can one minimize risk?* About 90% of fraud cases involve the employees of a company trying to exploit or steal money from the organization. This is why it is so important to have fraud prevention added to a company's plan. Such a plan entails the following:

Get to know employees

A company or business should take the time to get to know their employees. In the military, noncommissioned officers are encouraged to get to know who their soldiers are and what is going on within their families. When a company knows their employees, it is easy to observe their attitudes and behaviors for any changes that may indicate something is wrong. It is also important to know how they are feeling about their job and boss. These observations do not always stop fraud; however, they can give clues as to how to make changes to the organization and make it a better and happier place to work. This alone could discourage employee fraud.

Make employees aware and set up a system for reporting

Employee awareness is essential for fraud prevention. For example, for a huge corporation, it is hard to know everyone who works for them. However, all the employees know each other in their sections or work areas. Training employees to know what to look for will help to minimize the risk. At the same time, those employees who are thinking about fraud will know that it is a huge risk when everyone in the company from the management to the lowest employee is watching. The main reason why employees do not report what they see is because they are afraid the fraudulent employee will find out. That is why it is essential to have a reporting system that allows employees to report issues with anonymity.

Implement controls internally

Internal controls keep the assets of a company safe. One way to do this is the segregation of duties. The same person who is doing a company's accounting should not be allowed to write the checks and then turn around and sign them as the approving authority. This would make it easy for that person to steal funds from the company. Instead, there should be a different person appointed for each part of the operation. Thus, by the time the check is electronically sent to the employee, it has gone through at least three or more people to get full approval.

The segregation of duties also ensures everything is documented. This includes a note from every person an item goes through for it to be approved. It is much like the chain of command in the military. This paper trail will also go through a chain of command, and reflects the saying, 'If it is not in writing, it does not exist.'

Keep an eye on vacation days

Most employees need days off. However, in some instances, such days are red flags. A company or business should rotate employees to different areas periodically to give them a break and to reveal any fraud that may be going on. Cross training employees is a great way to help a company grow.

Hire an expert

Establishing procedures and policies can be tedious work, so a company may want to hire a professional, such as a forensic accountant, to help with this grueling task. A professional could be anyone who is certified as a Fraud Examiner or a Certified Public Accountant.

Embrace corporate culture and provide a positive place to work

The culture of an organization should be positive. This can help stop employees from committing fraud or theft. Many times, these crimes are due to a disgruntled employee. A company or business should always have everything black and white for the employees. The structure of the organization, the procedures, and the policies should be clear so that employees know where they stand. Having an open-door policy is a great way to show employees that the company is always accessible for them to come and discuss their issues. However, this only works if the company also take the initiative to listen to the issues and do something about them. Nobody wants to work in a place where they the "boss" is always on their case. Having a positive work environment is essential to the success of any organization.

Be the example

A true leader will set the example by *doing*. It does not matter where they are in the company; they should always be an example to employees and fellow workers. This includes following all the rules, procedures, and policies that are set by the company.

Create a policy manual

An organization should have a policy manual, and everyone who works for the company should either have easy access to it or a copy.

Have a code of conduct

A code of conduct is essential for all businesses. This allows employees to know and understand that there will be zero tolerance for any fraudulent activities. It should clearly state what is considered fraud. There should not be any room for guessing or gray areas.

Create a policy for Whistleblowers

The best eyes within a company are other employees. The issue most of them face is fear. They fear that the fraudulent individual will retaliate and come after them for saying something. Therefore, this policy is vital and can help stop fraud before it goes too far.

Review the Financials

It is important that there is a review and a reconciliation of all financial accounts. This will help a company or business to keep up-to-date on all records and makes it easier to detect if there is any fraud. Often, it will help to pinpoint which area the fraud is in and allow a company to catch it before it goes too far.

Incorporate a physical control of access

A company does not want everyone to get access to areas that do not pertain to their job. At the same time, a business may also want to control the access to specific areas that would be enticing to fraud. These areas include security systems, safes, computer systems, and cash registers.

There are so many regulators that a company can undertake concerning fraud prevention. The preceding list was just some chief examples. Management should take the time to meet and discuss what controls the given company requires to ensure that all the needs of the organization are met.

Chapter 9 – Technology and Tools Used

We live in a digital age of computers and technology. Granted, as life advances, so do crimes. Now, we are faced with digital crime, and our techniques and tools need to be upgraded to keep up with it.

Technology makes it easier to commit financial fraud. Most companies have all their financials online through "cloud" technology, and this can be placed into two categories: tool or target.

A forensic accountant performs thousands of investigations. In the world of the Internet, they must be equipped with tools of change. These tools need to consist of software for data mining and performing analysis. The following are a few examples of such tools:

Helix

This is a great Internet tool that is used to collect sound images from several different types of drives. This also includes partition drives that use a unique system setup like RAID arrays. Several systems offer the same service; however, this system is different as it is free and an open source.

Helix can be used as a forensic boot with x86 systems or as a live forensic image. When a computer is shut down, there is a good chance that evidence could be destroyed. Thus, a forensic examiner needs to be careful when shutting down a computer. The best way to shut down the computer, without risking the loss of data, is through unplugging it. Helix runs through the Linux side, and the system can be rebooted using Helix. Once this occurs, it will show the desktop with everything as a read-only. This will prevent the data from being altered in any way. The Helix system can be obtained from: **www.e-fense.com**

ACL Desktop

This system defines ACL as a useful tool that will also read well and analyze files. These files may be scattered through several databases throughout different platforms. It will give an immediate visual on data that is critical for an organization. This will allow analysis of all the data that is populated for complete assurance. This system could also show the following information:

- Trends
- Highlights and exceptions of potential areas that are of concern
- Any potential errors or fraud
- If there are any control issues and make sure the organization is following the standards and regulations
- And so much more

This system can be pricey. It can be found at: www.acl.com.

UltraBlock

Authentic documents and records are a must when submitted to the courts. It is very important for a forensic accountant not to alter any of their data. This is where UltraBlock comes in. This is a forensic write blocker hardware system. It makes it impossible for data to be changed. It is also compatible with other tools. However, it is also expensive. You can find this kit at: www.digitalintelligence.com

Passware Kit Forensic

This is a great tool that is used for the discovery of evidence reports that are password-protected on the computer that is being investigated. It will give access to items by using one of the fastest password and decryption recovery algorithms. This will allow the recovery of the strongest passwords. This system can be found at: www.lostpassword.com.

These are all great tools; however, they do not replace hard evidence and documents from outside sources. Anything that is obtained through these tools must be checked for authenticity. A forensic accountant does not want to go through all this work and have their documents not be accepted in court.

Chapter 10 – Lessons Learned

Forensic accounting has been around for centuries and has helped in some of the most prominent legal cases to date. Let's look back on some and see what made each case a success or a failure.

The Enron Scandal

This scandal is the most prominent case in American history and took place between the mid-1980s and 2001. Millions of dollars were hidden through projects that had failed and raked up debt. The scandal involved company executives and the accounting team working together to hide the money.

Enron had a creative team of accountants with skilled techniques. They worked hard to hide debt in the partnerships, misrepresent the money on the financial statements, and inflate the debt ratings and price stocks.

Through the acts of these leaders, the stock price for Enron crashed. It was at $90 per share and immediately dropped to $1 per share. This raised a huge red flag for the company. An investigation began where a forensic accountant dug up a lot of hidden information. The CEO, Jeff Skilling, was charged with several felonies and served fourteen years in prison. The former CEO, Kenneth Lay, was found guilty on ten counts of security fraud. He passed away before being sent to prison.

The WorldCom Fraud

With success in 1990, WorldCom was a company that worked in telecommunications. There was a proposed merger with Sprint; however, that was shut down by the United States Justice Department. The company struggled to stay alive after the decline in the industry in 2000.

The situation for WorldCom worsened. For them to keep their stock prices high, they turned to accounting methods that were fraudulent. This was to disguise what the company was really earning. Knowing the company was struggling, auditors worked around the clock to examine the financials of the company for fraud. These audits took months to complete, and the findings were astounding.

The auditors discovered $3.8 *billion*-plus fraudulent entries. They were found through recording lines incorrectly as capital expenditure. This caused an inflating revenue that was with fake revenue accounts that were unallocated. These findings were reported to the board's audit committee and the SEC.

What happened to WorldCom? They had to pay *millions* in penalties and was forced into bankruptcy. They are now operating as MCI Inc and is a subsidiary through Verizon.

The AIG Scandal

The fraud with the American International Group, Inc went from December 2000 to March 2001. AIG entered a series of transactions with Gen Re Corporation that were fraudulent. The purpose was to create a reinsurance policy that was false. This was to increase an appearance of AIG loss reserves and a report on the balance sheet to reflect that.

The investigation was at both the state and federal level. Forensic experts were on the trail for clues and eventually found the fraudulent transactions. Through a SEC investigation and a trial, AIG was guilty of accounting fraud. AIG was defrauding their analysts and investors. They also violated the policies set by the SEC and the GAAP.

AIG was fined $100,000,000. They also needed to make it right to their investors and were required to give $700,000,000 of their gains back to their investors.

Sir Paul McCartney and Heather Mills Divorce

This is one of the most famous divorce cases. During the divorce, the question was asked, *How much is this Beatle star really worth?* McCartney claimed that his net worth was about $400,000,000. Granted, Mills insisted that he was worth a lot more and considered it to be closer to $800,000,000.

Mills was determined to prove that she was right and hired a forensic accountant to seek out the truth. Keep in mind that she was technically entitled to half – now we see the real motive.

In the end, the judge ruled that McCartney was worth $450,000,000 in assets. This meant that $16,500,000 was awarded to Mills in the divorce.

Al Capone's Tax Evasion

Al Capone was considered one of the most famous gangsters of his time. He was legendary from 1920 to 1930. Somehow, he always managed to escape the law. *So how did you get convicted?* The answer is simple: through his accountant.

Based on the knowledge of this accountant, the experts were brought in, and through a lot of digging, the forensic accountants could found evidence of tax evasion. Thanks to this investigation, the IRS got involved and calculated what he brought in as earnings through his illegal activities that were not reported.

Thanks to one accountant being brave enough to go against his mob boss, Capone was imprisoned for eleven years. He was also required to pay back $215,000 in taxes and fined $50,000.

Due to this case with Capone, future law enforcement was given a way to convict crimes of tax evasion and additional tools to battle this ongoing issue.

Robert Maxwell's Embezzlement

For years, Robert Maxwell embezzled from his clients and shareholders. Maxwell was a European publisher who passed away in 1991. His company was built on lies and deception. He played a dangerous game playing with loans and findings for his business. Upon his death, the company crumbled.

It took an entire team of forensic accountants to decipher the records. This company was such a mess that it took fourteen years to find out that Maxwell had embezzled >$1 billion.

O.J. Simpson's Millions

Another big story was O.J. Simpson. Once Simpson received an innocent verdict, all the families of his victims filed a suit against him for financial compensation. He claimed to be broke and could not pay any money to the lawsuits.

It was hard to believe that Simpson was broke, so it wasn't surprising when forensic accountants began their investigation and later found that Simpson had millions hidden away. The families got $33,000,000 in settlements.

Although these only represent a small handful of cases, they show how a forensic accountant's specialized skills in accounting and investigating play a significant role in financial, legal cases.

Chapter 11 – Things to Remember

There is a lot of information in this book, so here are a few things to remember as you move towards a career in forensic accountancy.

Start with your education

Education is important, and most jobs require a bachelor's degree. Forensic accountants are no different. You will be required to have a Bachelor of Accounting. If you are not able to obtain this bachelor, consider a certification or start your degree with individual courses. This will be a great way to get your feet wet in accounting and to learn more about the world of forensic accounting.

Know what organization you want to work for

You should research whom you want to work with, and for, while you study. The goal is to have it figured out and apply as you complete your degree. There are several companies, businesses, and federal agencies you could work for after graduation. The real question is if you want to work in the private or public sector?

Work towards getting your CPA

You cannot get your CPA until you have your Bachelor of Accounting. However, to be a forensic accountant, you need to be a CPA. This is a prerequisite that the majority of companies require. Being a forensic accountant is not all about accounting though. There are additional skills needed. This would be a great time to further your learning into an interest that will tie into forensic accounting, such as investigative and legal skills. A great course to take would involve investigating fraud cases.

What area do you want to specialize in?

You are the expert and may want to specialize in a specific area that interests you. Some of these areas may be investigating criminal and fraud cases, cases of insolvency and bankruptcy, insurance claims, claims in personal injuries, disputes of matrimony, or cases of audit and valuations for business. Now is the perfect time to start researching these areas.

What are the responsibilities that are required?

A forensic accountant does more than just review the data they receive. Some of their additional responsibilities include but are not limited to:

➢ Planning investigations to the fullest of detail while outlining the methodology and goals.

➢ Taking financial data and creating models that will be used in an investigation.

➢ Tackling the scrutinizing research for complicated transactions.

➢ Quantifying any profits or losses.

➢ Writing and presenting reports along with additional documents.

➢ Assisting in creating and putting into effect procedures and processes.

➢ Mediating between various parties and assisting with the negotiations.

➢ Understanding the laws and rules regarding a case.

> Presenting evidence and testifying as an expert witness in court. This will allow them to explain methodologies to the judge and jury.

> Having a firm and clear understanding of the code of conduct and all the rules of evidence.

> Adhering and complying to the legislation as it is required.

You are a team player, not an individual rebel

A forensic accountant is a member of a team. This team is assigned to investigate a case. Each member has a specific job with a joint end goal. The team might consist of:

> A business or financial manager

> A document examiner

> business stakeholders, like a partner or investor

> A private investigator

> A forensic accountant

It is essential to be great at team-building. You will need to be comfortable working with others and possess the proper investigative and communication skills for the investigation.

Your communication skills must be on point

Communication is key to any job. With all the reports and trials that you will be involved in, this makes sense. As a forensic accountant, you need to go into it thinking no one knows the language you speak and it needs to be broken down as if you were teaching a child how to read and speak. Sometimes, you will have a case that is so complex that it needs to be thoroughly explained to a judge or jury in plain English, as they do not know legal or accounting terms.

Curiosity is important

Do not take things for granted. Just because it may look straightforward does not mean it is. The real clues are beneath the surface. Dig deep into the evidence you have and what you don't have. Question everything with a critical eye. You may need to think outside of the box. Go far beyond the normal techniques and perhaps invent your own to get the answers you seek.

The Seven Common Risks

There are seven common risks that a forensic accountant can alleviate:

#1 – A business' processes may become rigid and can conform to the thoughtless check-the-box approvals and reviews. The solution would be for a forensic accountant to implement the continuous audits of the controls that are critical.

#2 – Key nonfinancial and financial data is not comprehensively communicated, integrated and maintained to operations personnel promptly. The solution is to enhance the accounting information system by considering any potential dispute resolutions that are needed and include any long-term objectives.

#3 – Market and regulatory effects can cause changes in the responsibilities that are assigned to the agents and employees in that they do not follow through with them. The solution is to have a team of forensic accountants conduct an audit periodically of the human resource function to assess its capacity for managing performance and change.

#4 – A board of directors does not receive diverse, robust, and occasionally challenging consultation. The solution is to enhance the audit committee through an indirect liaison. This will be a supplement to the external auditing function.

#5 – Monitoring economic and human resources is a constraint by a legacy system, institutional or habitual inattentiveness, sunk cost, or other means. The solution is to reevaluate approaches that are potential conflicts or issues. This will increase the effectiveness of a forensic accounting team and activate their critical-thinking and problem-solving skills.

#6 – Strategies become inadequately informed, which results in financial engineering instead of economic growth. The solution is with a team of forensic accountants. They can plan a strategy, spot opportunities, and envision economic potential. Their skills are multi-discipline and combined with diverse experience makes them perfect for the job.

#7 – Talent development becomes mired in the employees' personal ambitions and fiefdom expansion. The solution is to examine the purpose and situational remedies. A forensic accountant is impartial, and their experiences in conducting rigorous analysis will be valuable.

These common risks are not typically addressed within a company, yet they might leave a business vulnerable to fraud and other crimes. It is hard to know all the risks that are involved in running a company. However, it is important to know how a forensic accountant can help in these high-risk areas.

It cannot be highlighted enough how important education is. When you are considered the 'expert in the field', that is what is expected. You always need to study and learn as much as you can. Along with getting your Bachelor of Accounting, you may want to pursue a Masters in Forensic Accounting, as well as take additional courses on some of the following areas:

- Ethics
- Statistics
- Criminology
- Business Law
- Psychology
- Business Writing

The aim is to take any course that will help you get a job and help in your investigations as a forensic accountant. Supplementary education looks excellent on a resume, but it looks even better when you actually put your skills to use for an investigation!

Chapter 12: How Internships Can Help You Break into Forensic Accounting

College students and those looking to go into a new career that has an abundance of job opportunities and growth potential, getting into forensic accounting is a great choice. While getting a job can be a challenge without experience, internships are a great way to get your foot in the business. If you are looking for a good forensic accounting internship, there are several steps that need to be followed in order to find the best fit for you.

Don't go into this thinking that you wouldn't be able to find an internship that will be just right for you. The fact is, there are internships out there that will suit anyone willing to learn and work hard. There is never a situation where all the doors are closed. Sometimes, you have to be willing to do a little digging to find the right internship. Having said that, it may not always be best to grab the first opportunity that comes your way. If you have several options, take the time to really think about each of them. It can be exciting to get opportunities, but you should avoid going into any of them blindly.

Using connections is important. Take the time to think about the people you know who can help you. Write down your friends and contracts, anyone who could know someone else who could help you. Then, let them know you are looking for an internship. Be open and honest about your search. There is nothing wrong with asking for help. Chances are, you will get positive leads. They might not always work out, but the interviewing experience and the opportunity to meet industry professionals are always valuable.

The most important thing is to start early. The best forensic accounting internships will be competitive, and sometimes, you can be given preference if you start the process far in advance. If you are seeking a summer internship, the process will typically start with the application process during the fall. That is about six months prior to the summer in question. Most people wouldn't think that the process would start so soon, and as a consequence, they aren't prepared. If you know that you would like to get into an internship in the near future, start looking for one as soon as possible. If you are currently in college, this is a great time to check out your school's career counseling center. They will most likely have a great set of resources, and sometimes, they'd even have opportunities exclusive to the students of your school. You can also get the established application timelines for internships from them.

The next step is to really think about how forensic accounting compares to other accounting fields. Use this book to fully comprehend your career steps and outlook. If you understand the ins and outs of the industry, it will be much easier to feel prepared as you go into your internship. Having a full knowledge of and interest in the forensic accounting field and being able to express that to interviewers are just a couple of great ways to seem more striking to employers.

Once you have all the information, the next thing to do is to practice your interviewing skills. In order to do everything you can to get the job you want, you need to practice. If you don't have a lot of job experience, you probably don't have a lot of experience with interviews either. Not practicing can make you appear unprepared or lacking in knowledge, so take the time to refine your interview skills.

Practicing is pretty simple. Have a friend or family member act as your interviewer and ask you common interview questions until you can answer them all smoothly. Again, if you are currently enrolled in or an alumni of a university, the career center can be a great resource. Many of them have professionals on staff who can give you a mock interview and feedback based on your performance, and you can use this experience to improve and to help you feel more confident before you step into your real interview.

Even if you do have experience interviewing and getting jobs, it never hurts to practice. You can have someone prepare tough or complicated questions to take your interview skills to a whole new level.

The next thing to do is to follow up, and you should do so at least three times. The first time, do it on the same day as your interview. Note, however, that you shouldn't necessarily ask about the position. What you'll want to do is thank them for their time. You should try and inject a portion of the interview back into the thank-you email. This isn't as hard as it may seem, and it can help you stand out. If they asked you a question you didn't know the answer to or about a technology you weren't familiar with, do your research and include what you learned in your email.

Here's an example: "In our conversation, we had the opportunity to speak about Benford's Law. Through my research, I learned how important this principle is in analyzing the validity of forensic records."

This shows that you are a passionate learner and that you really care about the specific internship and forensic accounting in general. The next two follow-ups should be spaced two weeks apart. They should express enthusiasm for the position, and you should ask if there is anything you need to provide or anything that you could do to further show your potential as a candidate.

They should never appear hostile or angry, only positive and excited. Having an internship is something that can really help your career in the best ways, so try to follow the logical steps to achieve your goals. It is important that you never give up. The next opportunity could be *your* opportunity, and if forensic accounting is for you, go for it!

Once you get that internship, you will, of course, need to do well. Let's talk about some ways you can do just that.

Getting an internship means you will be getting valuable experience in the field of forensic accounting. It will put you in a position to learn if you have what it takes and if it really is the job for you. You will be challenged and may end up confused, but you will also grow in a short amount of time. Many times, internships last only a month or two, but they can feel like a lifetime. That is what makes internships great.

Once you have acquired an internship, take the time to be as prepared as you can for your first day. Wear the appropriate work attire, which is typically business professional or business casual. Here's a tip: during your interview, take note of the dress code and be prepared to match it. Have a good breakfast and be there half an hour early. This will keep you calm and centered for your first day. When you meet your co-workers, stay positive and confident. Take in everything you can. They know that you are there to learn and work hard, so do just that.

Be prepared to learn all you can. Internships and learning go together inextricably. In the best case scenario, the firm you work for will trust you to complete real, legitimate work and teach you in the process. This is an incredibly exciting opportunity to get your feet wet with complex work. The level of complexity or importance of your work will be different based on your firm and supervisor. The hope is that you can work on some really great projects. Those projects could give you a real glimpse of what it's like to be a forensic accountant. Also, once you've spent a good amount of time learning, try to seek out opportunities for extra responsibilities. That enthusiasm might very well land you a new job!

Occupational fraud is a serious type of fraud that costs businesses in the USA more than 50 billion dollars every year. A third of that amount is due to direct employee theft. It is estimated that three-fourths of all employees have stolen from their place of employment, and of that portion, at least half have stolen repeatedly. That includes both small-scale and large-scale theft, and it is such a pervasive problem for employers. The average loss from occupational fraud is about $140,000 per incident, and the fraud lasts an average of 18 months. That comes up to an estimated 5% loss in revenue each year.

It doesn't just affect large businesses. In fact, businesses with 100 employees or less account for a big chunk of all occupational fraud cases. Most fraudsters are never charged or convicted of fraud-related offenses. The fraudsters often stay in the company long-term, and over half of them stay employed by their company for more than six years. Due to their small revenue streams, small businesses will experience a larger average loss. As such, forensic accountants might serve small businesses even better than larger ones and save them a large amount of money.

If you're in the banking or financial industry, your business is in the sector that has the most incidences of fraud. There are reasons for this. A third of the organizations that are victims of fraud have no internal controls, and that portion is much bigger for small businesses. Anonymous tips are the most common way companies get information, and most companies rely on these to get information about potential fraud.

The size or type of a company cannot keep it safe from fraud. Any company without forensic accountants and good internal controls is just waiting to receive their losses. Even if you do have good internal controls, they need to regularly be assessed and altered as necessary.

There are three major types of occupational fraud. The first type is asset misappropriation schemes. It is by far the most common form of fraud, but they result in the smallest financial loss. This is any kind of theft or misappropriation of the company resources. Examples of this include check tampering, skimming, cash register disbursements, and payroll fraud.

The second type of occupational fraud is corruption schemes. This is a little more complex than your average asset misappropriation schemes. This type of fraud is where employees misuse their influence in business transactions. They do this to gain some type of benefit both directly and indirectly. The way an employee uses their influence violates their duty to their company. Examples of corruption schemes include bid rigging, wherein the bidding on a project gets unfairly skewed because of unauthorized side deals.

Financial statement fraud schemes are the third type of occupational fraud. This is when an employee intentionally omits or alters material information on a company's financial reports. Some examples include inaccurate revenues or inflating assets on reports. This is a pretty rare kind of occupational fraud, but it is very much more expensive than any other type.

Having internal controls is so important. Internal control is a process that is affected by every companies' board of directors as well as the management and other essential personnel. It is designed to provide safeguards against fraud by establishing standards in three categories: reliability of financial reporting, compliance with regulations and laws, and effectiveness and efficiency of operations.

Reliability of financial reporting pertains to how a company prepares reliable and true financial statements. Compliance with regulations and law is the process of dealing with and complying with regulations and laws to which a business is subject under. Effectiveness and efficiency of operations simply means that a company's business objectives work well for the company itself.

Chapter 13: Internal Control Policies

Now, let's focus on control policies and procedures specifically. Let's see how an organization can implement them in order to ensure the safety of company resources.

The implementation of internal controls can be a costly endeavor, but there are steps you can take to minimize your company's risk without using up too many resources. These steps can be great for early detection as well as prevention. Sometimes, you won't even need to change your process as a whole. You may just need to add a few steps to an existing process or even redistribute job responsibilities such that no dramatic changes have to be made. For example, you can change employee duties in order to stay ahead of the curve. Fraud is such an ever-changing element, so we have to change with it. Adding a few elements here and there over time can make a big difference for your business.

In order to figure out where to make changes, you have to consider where a company is most vulnerable. The answer may or may not be obvious, going by the money that is received and dispersed in the bank accounts of the firms.

The easiest procedure for you to implement related to receiving money is a separation of duties. This is a process that is easier to implement if you are a larger company with many employees, but even for smaller business, it can still be applied. Some alternatives also include the owner's involvement in reviewing the accounting information.

To implement separation of duties, start with those in charge of the banking responsibilities. Modify your process so that only one person in a billing office issues the invoices and another person in another office receives and deposits the money. This separates the money in and money out, eliminating any possibility of one person being in charge of both.

Another control policy to implement is to have bank accounts reconciliation take place in a third office. The most important element in bank accounts reconciliation is verifying the cleared checks that have been posted in the ledger. If it doesn't show in the ledger, it's the forensic accountant's job to investigate. When everything is separate and one person only handles one function in the banking, the whole process becomes very smooth. In receivables, one office handles disbursement and another reconciles bank accounts.

Many companies will have an employee that handles both the wire transfer and payables. Following are a few procedures to implement. After a check or wire has been set up, an owner or partner has to approve the funds. This ensures that money only goes to legitimate sources—not family, friends, or a fake person altogether. There is a tool called Positive Pay. It allows a bank to be pre-notified about all the checks that were written so they can be pre-approved as they are presented. This way, a bank will only accept approved checks from your company. This is a great process because it protects the company against frauds like check duplication.

Additionally, if a check should have been approved but wasn't, the bank can simply give the company a call and request approval from a partner verbally. This not only increases the review of checks that employees prepare, it guards the firm against anyone duplicating checks or cleaning out business accounts without your consent. For example, someone could duplicate your checks and write one to themselves and cash it without approval. Another internal control is a partner whose job is to reconcile the checkbook. If they notice a check to an unfamiliar vendor, they should investigate and call in a forensic accountant. This action can save your business a lot of money and countless hours.

When working in a company, make sure to always review the bank statements and cleared checks. Compare signatures—if the signatures from the same person are very different, there might be something wrong. Typically, signatures are always signed in the same place as well. If they are not in almost the exact same place, there is probably a problem.

An interesting way that the insurance industry has really expanded in the last few years is through the introduction of the "expert fee fund." This is where an accounting firm disperses funds on behalf of insurance carriers. They will then receive the expert fee invoices, and they will pay for each case after review.

As this happens more and more, there would have to be standards put in place to ensure that no money will be misplaced or stolen. One way to keep money where it should be is to use a trust account. These accounts are specifically designed to prevent fraud. In the next paragraphs, we will discuss some protocols to prevent theft when employees and partners have the ability to disburse funds, very similar to the attorney trust account.

The way one protocol works is that two partners will act as assignors and no employees will have the authority to sign checks. The partners will be responsible for payment requests and things like providing copies of the invoice and verification of identification. A partner should be able to reconcile the account and look for any payments that seem out of place. This process is very similar to the separation of duties.

Another type of audit is a documentation audit. It should occur only occasionally for verifying that all disbursements are valid. While the procedures may be similar, the difference between this and trusts is the circumstances in which they are to be implemented.

While trust accounts are slightly different from each other, similar procedures may be utilized. Similarly, as every circumstance and account is different, the above can be used as a guide that can be modified as appropriate to each account and firm's requirements.

Chapter 14: A Few Common Examples of General Fraud

A form of fraud uses what are called "ghost employees." This is where an employee sets up an employee entry in the payroll. Then, the money that the fake employee receives goes into an account that the fraudster controls. To prevent this serious action, make sure that only one person in one office is doing all of your payroll functions. Once or twice a month, the payroll register should be reviewed for fictional employees or any inconsistencies in pay. This should be done by a partner in an unrelated office. Note that while this is a great process, it is really only feasible if you have less than 100 employees. If you have more than 100 employees and a payroll officer who aren't familiar with each one, this is much harder to implement effectively. If this is the case, you can look for large-scale amounts or odd payroll registration and investigate those.

The expense account of a company is one of the most vulnerable to fraud. There are some steps you can take to keep track of spending and only accept legitimate transactions. One of the easier ways is to give a corporate credit card to all eligible partners and employees. All the cards will be billed to a singular master account that is paid by the company. This puts all the transactions in one place for review and ensures that all the expenses have been accounted for in the expense account. It will be easy to find if something is out of place, and any misappropriations can be addressed.

Expense reconciliation should happen every month. If there are unreported expenses, the employee responsible for them should be questioned and the expenses should be reported. Every quarter, the expenses should be scanned. Look for anything that strikes you as odd and investigate as needed. Even if no fraudulent charges ever appear, it is important to take these extra steps. Having employees know the lengths you will take to protect the business' earnings will have them think twice about attempting anything.

There are many organizations that let employees use their own personal credit cards for travel and other expenses. This is can be an ineffective way to protect company assets. For example, let's say that an employee buys a plane ticket that costs $1000. They then show the receipt to their company and get reimbursed, but what is to stop that employee from getting a refund on $1000 plane ticket, purchasing a cheaper flight, and pocketing the extra money? There is absolutely no way for a business to verify if this was or was not done. The only way to verify payment is to get the employee to show personal credit card records, something most employees would absolutely refuse to do. If everyone uses a corporate card, on the other hand, this would not be an issue. The company would see the credit and only pay for what is actually getting used. This is an essential element for any business.

To ensure your company will not fall victim to any of the examples of fraud laid out in this book, you should be stringent when setting measures in place. A simple method is to bring in a professional from outside who could interview employees as well as analyze the internal controls based on your business' individual needs and the amount of staff you have. One other benefit is that a forensic accountant who is an outsider can look at things within your company with fresh eyes. Sometimes, it is easy to ignore faults when they are your own. They can also judge each employees' response to questioning and figure out what those responses mean. Additionally, you can have a partner do a money review of the financial documents. This will ensure that nothing obviously outside of the norm is happening.

Never cut corners when it comes to internal controls. A little extra effort can go a really long way. It may not seem like an interesting point to brag about with shareholders, but it's a lot better than having to explain to those same people why a fraud occurred.

There are so many ways a forensic accountant can be useful. Let us look at some of the less common ways a business can benefit from having one on board.

In partnership and shareholding disputes, compensation and benefits are typical issues. There is usually a dispute about the amount or the agreement about those amounts. A forensic accountant will be able to look at the financial documents with a kind of legal scrutiny that will allow the dispute to reach a conclusion. They can prove who is the correct party so that everyone can move forward.

Insurance claims are another area for which forensic accountants can be very useful. Insurance companies have policies that are incredibly different from those laid out in their terms and conditions. Sometimes, they can even seem intentionally misleading. It is so important to be able to calculate the economic damage in settlement claims. These cases are not easy to solve—they will need to do an extensive analysis of the policy to understand the issues with coverage.

A forensic accountant could be brought in to help either the insurance company or the insurer themselves. They will come in and conduct an investigation and then help the parties come up with a proper settlement of the case. In a business environment, the types of assignments may include business losses or employee fidelity claims.

Economic losses is another place where a forensic accountant can be of great use. The issues in these cases usually include construction claims, trademark and patent infringements, and product liability claims due to the breach of a non-compete agreement. Forensic accountants will take a deeper look at the different terms and conditions. Then, they will look at how the circumstances that led up to the current dispute occurred. After that, they will put a number on any substantiated losses involved in the dispute.

Personal insurance is another sector where a forensic accountant can be of service. Forensic accountants will find that their services for the insurance realm can be given to personal uses as well. Forensic accountants have the specific ability to put a number on any economic damages that come from a medical incident. Many times, forensic investigation is the preferred method because it will provide an in-depth understanding of the legislative process, especially regarding the settlement claims that occur in these types of cases. They will review the insurance policies, report any issues with coverage, and then employ methodologies to calculate the potential loses.

Chapter 15: Auditing and Forensic Accounting

Auditing is an important element of forensic accounting and accounting in general. An audit is a complete and thorough review of any company's financial records. These audits are done by external auditors. This establishes that the audit is both reliable and accurate.

Audits are typically done to elevate compliance processes and ensure everything is within regulation. These kinds of independent audits are conducted to provide the company with assurance that the financial statements are correct and that the company is not being defrauded. If your company ever wants to be awarded government contracts, you will have to submit to a government audit. These are done to verify that a potential contractor actually has internal controls and that they are effective in discouraging fraud in that workplace. There are many resources that your company could use to learn about proper policies and procedures, and this book is among them. Another great place to find information is the American Institute of Certified Public Accountants. They have published standards online free for anyone to use and follow.

There are several different types of audits, and there is a significant difference between external and internal audits. An internal auditor's job is to make sure that the internal controls are effective. They always need to be functional, and a full-time internal auditor's job is to make sure that everything is working smoothly. They have the task of auditing continuously, and that involves monitoring information on a real-time basis. They use computer software systems to audit the information quickly. There is also advanced software that uses data samples and analysis to find any suspicious patterns or inaccuracies.

The difference between traditional audits and forensic accounting audits is the intention. Traditional audits look for mistakes and inaccuracies, not outright fraud. They will not pursue an investigation for a small amount of missing money or a clear mistake. This is totally different from when a forensic accountant audits. They do not have a policy for overlooking cases with small inconsistencies. They have to throw away some of the accepted accounting concepts because they need to pursue everything. They believe that any inconsistency can be considered the smoke that will lead to the fire. They have to hunt down every lead.

Fraud auditors are forensic accountant partners. If they do not start an investigation, a forensic accountant will never be brought in. It all starts with a referral for what is called a fraud audit, but it could also be from an employee tip. A referral could be initiated due to any number of red flags. These red flags include unusual payments or anything that sticks out as out of the ordinary. After any kind of possible fraud is discovered, forensic accountants have to start working to find the source.

The major difference between fraud auditors and forensic accountants are the methods they use. Forensic auditing is what is called non-adversarial. They are looking for anything unusual, but no fraud has necessarily been found. Forensic accounting is adversarial because they would be pursuing an individual that is suspected of fraud.

While forensic accounting has some wonderful benefits, it does also have disadvantages. However, "disadvantage" may be too strong a word. A better one might be "roadblock," or perhaps even "disruptions." Forensic accounting is a long and sometimes cumbersome process. It involves a very intelligent person putting in the work, complete with the technical knowledge to put diverse pieces together.

Confidentiality can be a problem when hiring a forensic accountant. They are external people who will be looking at all the company's books. This could lead to confidential matters not staying that way. Now, forensic accountants are, as a whole, ethical people dedicated to confidentiality, but you could get a bad apple now and then. An isolated breach of trust can happen, and once those confidential details are out, you cannot take them back.

Having a forensic accountant on staff isn't cheap. Depending on how long they work, you could be on the hook for a huge expense. For big organizations, this is a necessary cost that most likely won't make a dent in resources. For small businesses, however, the cost might not be attainable. They could find it very difficult to find the funds. Plus, it doesn't stop with the accountant—you will be responsible for any high-end software they use and the legal fees associated with getting the forensic accountant in court to testify.

Bringing in a forensic accountant can be a double-edged sword. It can be a significant morale-buster for employees. Bringing in a forensic accountant is like throwing a living, breathing accusation at them. They could feel attacked before the forensic accountant can introduce themselves. Having employees who feel distrusted wouldn't make for a good working environment. Additionally, work can get delayed due to the necessary interviews and the other things employees will need to do when cooperating with a forensic accountant.

The people hiring forensic accountants always hope that they will find nothing. If they did happen to find someone who can be charged with a crime, that employee may attempt or threaten to defame the company to avoid persecution. If that happens, the company will be between a rock and a hard place. There's also the fact that the company must report whatever issues were found to shareholders and other outsiders, and this can really affect the business. A company might decide it's better to just not know.

Chapter 16: Obtaining a Forensic Accountant Masters Degree

You will learn many different things when you decide to pursue a forensic accountant master's degree. This program will give you the chance to develop and hone your skills. It will help you become a more confident professional. Your training will also meet the requirements for a forensic accounting certification, and these classes will help you know how to look beyond the numbers and see the whole picture of a business. Seeing the whole picture will enable you to find patterns and potentially fraudulent transactions. You will also be able to provide excellent financial analysis for those who may not have an understanding of accounting.

Forensic accounts look at the patterns and then work to understand them. This is what all kinds of investigators do. A lot of what forensic accountants do is the same thing investigators have always done, but now, technology plays a huge role in how those patterns are found. A good forensic accounting program would spend a lot of time helping you develop data collection skills as well as data visualization on data analytics. You'll want to find a program that is technology-forward. These are the tools you'll use in the real world, so you'll need to learn them in your master's program.

A good masters program will have real-life case studies to review and ways for you to practice forensic audits as well as internal and external ones. You'll have the opportunity to practice looking into companies' finances for any sign or fraud or insulation. A good example of this would be looking at the receipts from rent payments and figuring out if they fit the description or if there's a breach of contract. You might look at internal audits and critique a company's internal controls, policies, and procedures. You should also get a lot of practice with external audits, which would be like fact-checking allegations to give them credibility.

There should also be an emphasis on legal studies because, while the legal portion of the job is very important, it is easy to overlook. Forensic accountants have to understand legal definitions and concepts. This is true for both criminal as well as the civil court. The civil and criminal court can differ extensively. As was discussed in other sections of the book, your job as a forensic accountant will be to break down the complex financial, accounting, or legal concepts to people who don't understand them. Many masters programs will actually train you in the art of giving court testimony, and these will feature mock trials and court visits.

In order to become a forensic accountant, you have to be comfortable with different software programs like Excel, Word, and PowerPoint, as you'll use them a lot for analyzing and gathering information. You will also need to be very knowledgeable in computer software programs because those will be needed for analyzing and gathering information. Job candidates have to be able to research online and use the database management software that the company does.

Ethics will always play a huge role in forensic accounting. You will need to always walk with a lot of personal integrity. Every time you speak at work, you must do so in a thoroughly honest manner. You are also going to have to clear a background check. Many jobs will expect you to be able to get a security clearance, so clean up your internet presence and keep out of any legal trouble and bad debt.

Team-playing is important for forensic accountants They have to collaborate with co-workers and other employees using a high level of professionalism. After all, they are also responsible for reviewing documents and finding places where things and processes can be approved and financial reparations can be made.

There are several steps to follow to become a forensic accountant. Getting your bachelor's degree is the first step. Another educational step would be to get a CFF credential. Lastly, your certification program should include a certain set of knowledge bases. Let's take a look at these.

First, you'll need 75 hours of qualifying experience. You'll need to learn many skills, including the practice of gathering information, planning forensic engagement, and interviewing protocols, as well as report creation and the proper way to provide court testimony. After completing your certification program, you will officially be certified to work in the following areas:

- Reorganizations
- Misrepresentation of financial statements
- Family law
- Bankruptcies
- Insolvencies
- Technical forensic analyses
- Family law
- Preventing and detecting fraud

Having a bachelor's or master's degrees is a requirement for employment for many employers. Many will expect for these degrees to come from any one of these fields: finance, general accounting, and forensic accounting. Graduates who are looking for a way to stand out could find it beneficial to become CFO certified. It will tell employers that you can go the extra mile.

As a forensic accountant, you have to be proficient in analytical theories. This means understanding the different fraudulent methods in acquiring funds to be able to solve a white-collar crime.

Embezzlement schemes and money laundering, as well as hidden assets, are not easy to find, so forensic accountants will need to be highly skilled in their pursuits. Government regulations are another thing officials will need to know.

Forensic accountants are still accountants, but their salary and career path are more elevated. You can work in the typical places and businesses that most accountants go for, but that is just the beginning for you. There will be many other high-paying opportunities for forensic accountants. For example, forensic accountants are in high demand in government offices such as the SEC; their job there is to find fraud in all its forms.

One of the best things about becoming a forensic accountant is that it doesn't require you to complete a separate degree. If you already have a degree in accounting, you can very easily qualify for promotions and higher wages by taking extra coursework and becoming a certified forensic accountant.

You might think one of two ways about forensic accountants: they are either glorified paper pushers or they are detectives. The truth is, they are neither. Forensic accountants are a mix of both—sometimes, they are analyzing paperwork but, as discussed in this book, they are also armed with interpersonal skills that enable them to investigate people properly and find those who are potential fraudsters.

Chapter 17: Tools Forensic Accountants May Use

It comes as no surprise that basic accounting skills are the first tool that accountants may use. Hiding money is a very common method of committing financial crimes. You'll need basic accounting skills in order to find and track the money flow. For example, many financial crimes involve sheltering money in off-shore accounts or moving assets around so that people can avoid taxation.

Then there are technology tools. Software programs can definitely save thousands of man-hours. These tools can compile different kinds of data and help you identify any pattern. They can, for example, look for a large number of transactions that fall right under the threshold for a flag or for too many partial payments from customers.

Analytical tools are also important for forensic accountants, and one example that is often used is Benford's Law. This law states that numbers that are fraudulent have a different distribution from legitimate numbers. For example, "one" appears as the first digit about thirty percent of the time in legitimate accounting data. If the number one appears as the first digit more than half the time, it indicates potential fraud.

In no way should a forensic accountant rely on just one analytical tool to prove a financial crime. Software can help you identify a potent fraud pattern, but you will have to check the books and follow the pattern yourself. You will rely on so many factors, so you should use as many tools as you can to check your data.

Let's take a look at other tools that should be in your arsenal as a forensic accountant. These can all work together to make you a highly effective and accurate forensic accountant.

Duplicate checking is a process used to find the common fraud of sending duplicate checks to known individuals such as vendors but altering the address so that a person other than the vendor can cash the check. They may also collude with the vendor such that the vendor cashes the duplicate check and splits the profit. It is important to identify any duplicate values in the payment records. If you discover any, it needs to be investigated immediately.

Beneish's ratios is another analytical tool. It was created by Professor Messod Beneish of Indiana University. His research focused on the differences between the financial information of public companies that misrepresented their financial statements and of those that did not. There are eight ratios, or indexes, in the Beneish model. They look at many different elements of a financial statement and can help predict if a company has the potential to defraud any investors or lenders. Among others, those ratios look at the proportion of non-current assets to total assets, gross margin, and sales growth. All the ratios will be higher for companies intending to commit fraud.

The relative size factor is a ratio that is commonly used in forensic accounting. This is the ratio of the biggest number to the second biggest one in a dataset. This is a technique to determine the highest number in a dataset and to reference the second highest number. If there are any outliers, they are often investigated.

Data mining techniques are programs designed for scanning through large amounts of data. They are used when looking for anything that is unexpected or new and for implicit patterns or information; this program does all of this automatically. There are three data mining techniques. The first is the discovery method of data mining, the second is the predictive modeling and deviation, and the third is link analysis.

Geocoding is a tool that helps forensic accountants find shell companies. Shell companies are corporations that were established with the sole purpose of hiding a flow of funds from a defrauded company to the person perpetrating the fraud. It is really hard to follow this money trail because businesses write big checks every day. For a fraudster to even attempt to add their shell company as a vendor on the list, they have to feel confident that no one would notice, meaning there are many other transactions going on. Geocoding works by converting every street address connected to a vendor into a code that a mapping program can identify. Using geocoding means that you can visually see where every check was sent to individually. There, you can see breaks in the common patterns of addressing. A common example is a mailing address that is actually in a residential development.

Psychology is a tool that a forensic accountant will use every day. They may see red flags if the behavior of a particular member of the company is behaving unusually compared with their typical behavior. Let's look at some examples. Someone who is committing a financial crime may suddenly offer to do overtime, or perhaps stay late to do a job they would typically avoid. They may simply be looking for an excuse to spend time alone in the office. The suspect may also become very angry at small changes like office location or hours because these might expose their criminal activity. Many fraudsters will eventually spend an amount of money inconsistent with their salaries, and this will be a huge red flag. An employee who makes less than $30,000 a year can't possibly afford a $100,000 car. If those purchases become a pattern, you may have some suspicious activity going on.

Chapter 18: The Skills a Forensic Accountant Needs

The exact mix of what it takes to become a forensic accountant has very much been a subject of debate for a long time. Some people really believe in having strong educational backgrounds. They think that if you have the knowledge, you are bound to be successful. Others think that long-term experience is really what is needed for success. Whichever side they may be on, however, many people can agree that there are specific personality traits that every forensic accountant needs to possess in order to be successful.

Analytical thinking works in the favor of every forensic accountant. You'll need to analyze financial data and any other documents or evidence. To be successful, you'll need to be able to really scrutinize data and documents to understand if they are accurate, valid, and authentic.

Always look into the details. Those details matter more than anything else. In forensic accountancy, you have to be able to see not only the whole picture but also the details that make up the whole picture. If you ignore what may seem like a small or insignificant detail, you may end up derailing the whole investigative process.

Ethics are very important in forensic accounting. You will need to rely solely on proven facts and figures. You will need to evaluate data free of any personal opinion and emotions. You cannot let personal considerations influence any part of the investigation. If you do, your investigation will be invalid and no one would be able to trust your findings. Evaluate all information ethically, every time.

You will need to be insightful. This means you'll need to make intelligent observations that many people would typically overlook, and this is a very valuable trait in a forensic accountant.

Being persistent is also essential. It takes time to sort out an investigation. You'll need to gain access to confidential financial information, and that entails talking to the right people, sometimes many times. You cannot just quit on a theory until you are disproven—or proven right.

Next, you'll need to have a healthy dose of skepticism. You cannot just take the first answer that someone gives you. You will need to verify the information from more than one source. If you can't fact-check the information, it will simply stay as an unproven theory.

There cannot be a forensic accountant who doesn't have confidence. You'll need to trust your gut. You'll also have to know that your presence won't be welcome. To most others, you will be bad news walking. People assume that they will be getting into trouble, or worse, losing their jobs. That can make you feel unsettled, and you would not be able to do your job well if you don't feel comfortable.

You'll need to be inquisitive. Not only do you need to identify details, you need the kind of nature that wants to find the truth in those details. You'll need to be an investigator at heart. This means questioning everything and having the determination to find the real answers.

Oral and written communication skills are very important while gathering information and speaking to people with varying levels of understanding. In an investigation, there needs to be a flow of information created by forensic accountants. They have to be the one to put together what happens. Some experts suggest that forensic accountants should take any opportunity to develop their communication skills, including creating and delivering presentations. Some others suggest seeking professional training in public speaking. There is a lot of value in mentoring, team building, and training to improve the communication of critical information. It is important to be able to organize issues and focus on individual ones in your communication. Never forget to always make team building a major focus. There are programs that could help forensic accountants build rapport and trust within a team. They can also help you understand your strengths and weaknesses in how you communicate.

You will need to be agile and adaptable as you investigate. This investigation will more than likely make you change your work plan or make the entire workplace obsolete. If that happens, you'll need to start from scratch. You need to be able to think on your feet, so make "change" your new best friend.

Start seeing yourself as a problem solver first and foremost. Investigations in forensic accounting are similar to puzzles. Instead of this puzzle coming on a box with a picture guide, however, you get the pieces in a mesh bag. You'll need to figure out not only which piece goes where but also if there are pieces in the bag that don't belong in the bag at all. All in all, solving it will require a large amount of patience and dedication.

Improving your soft skills is just as important as improving your hard skills. It takes time and a lot of effort. But these are the skills that will help your investigations go smoothly and help you deal with stressful situations with other employees.

You should be able to interview people and get the best information out of them. During disputes and investigations, those being interviewed may feel that they are being accused of something or that they will lose their job even when they have nothing to hide. Forensic accountants have to help them feel comfortable. There should be a calm and welcoming environment when you interview someone. You should always be polite. It will help you get more meaningful information when the person is relaxed enough to talk. Be upfront and direct in your speech so that no one feels misunderstood. It is all about giving and getting the very best in the interviews.

Everyone needs to feel as comfortable as possible, even in an obviously stressful situation. You should also be really empathetic and listen to their concerns. Then, ask the questions you need to be answered. Most of the time, it is not *what* you say but simply *how* you say it that is the problem. Remember, too, that it is not how much you talk, it is how much you are willing to *listen* that will determine how much good information you can extract.

One last important thing to remember is to develop relationships prior to interviewing people. People are way more likely to talk to their friends rather than strangers. Get involved in the day to day of the office—get to know the people whose role is to face clients. You should integrate yourself into the real environment and office to help ensure your investigation will be a success.

Chapter 19: Studying for the CPA

First, do not try to avoid purchasing a review course. It is necessary. Taking the CPA without having any materials to study is like trying to do a task with both hands tied behind your back. Sure, you could use your other body parts to try to complete the task, but the chances of success will be very low if you try to do so. Make sure to do all the research you can on the review course. Pick the one that will help you learn the best and retain the information you will need.

There are so many different courses to choose from. They will all have different measurements of success and information retention. Some will offer you recommendations on what to study next or what to focus on. Some are so simple that they will only provide you the information and it is up to you to read and study the materials. Take advantage of any free trials that are being offered. At the very least, these could give you the opportunity to see if a review course will work well for you.

Keep the fact that you are studying to yourself. If your friends and family learn that you are studying for the exam, they may try to help or become very involved. That can add a lot of sadness and frustration if you need to cancel your exam or if you don't pass. You will have to make an announcement and explain what happened, then listen to the opinions of others. That makes this whole thing even more terrible. It will add a lot of pressure to the whole process, and where possible, pressure is best avoided.

Make sure you aren't only using multiple-choice questions to study for the CPA exam. You don't need to practice guessing, which is what multiple-choice practice questions can encourage. Instead, focus on learning the material presented. Try to understand the reasons you got the answers right or wrong.

Every CPA exam has what are called tasked-based simulations. These are case studies, and they allow candidates to show their knowledge and skills by responding to real-life situations instead of just choosing the right answer among a list. In other words, task-based simulations will really challenge you in acquiring the skills a CPA needs in the real world. In your practice and review, make sure to practice many tasked-based simulations.

Figure out your time of maximum productivity. It is important to know if you are a morning, day, or night person. This is helpful because knowing this information will help you craft the perfect study schedule, and it will also tell you the best time to schedule the CPA exam. If you are a morning person, waiting until the evening could cause anxiety and make you less cool-headed. It also works the other way around. Don't plan on taking an early morning test if you struggle with waking up. You'll be less focused which isn't good for your chances of passing.

It is perfectly fine to schedule your test last minute. Some people think you need to schedule your test very far in advance, and this is mostly to keep the pressure on and motivate you to study. This can be a terrible strategy. Instead of keeping up with your schedule, you'll end up getting behind and going into the exam unprepared resulting in a no-pass. Avoid that path and schedule the exam when you are actually ready to sit for it.

There is an exception to that rule. If you live in a town with only one testing center or where seats fill up fast, you may have to schedule early. A thing to keep in mind if you really don't want to schedule early is that people tend to cancel their test if they feel unprepared. Keep checking the site to check for open seats.

Remember the little victories. If you are studying for the CPA, chances are you'll be a little stressed and that can make you too hard on yourself. Make sure to reward yourself with a little fun! There is a sample study schedule below, and Sundays are completely open on it. Take your Sundays and make the most out of them. Get out and do the things you love with the people that make you happy.

Also, once you pass one section of the CPA exam, take a little time and celebrate properly before you go on to the next. There are some really great ways to celebrate in a big way. Plan a weekend trip to the beach, a shopping spree, dinner with friends, or a trip to the spa.

If you think that a lack of confidence during the exam will cause you to fail, think again. If you have the knowledge, it will show on the exam. Try your best to stay positive. Remember that the exam has pre-test questions, and if you come across one, it may very well be one of those questions that won't count against your score. Remember as well that the test is intuitive. The better you are doing, the harder it gets. If you are feeling more challenged, then you are most likely doing something very right!

Don't forget that you are on a time schedule to finish all three sections of the CPA exams. You will need to take the other three sections within 18 months. That may sound like a really long time, but it will run out quickly if you are not working toward it. Include that stretch of time in your study strategy. You cannot afford to waste any of it.

Keep your study schedule steady. You cannot study now and then or here and there. You have to have a dedicated mindset. If you don't, success won't be easy to attain. You have to set a plan and then treat it like it is an unmovable part of your life. Then, think about your study style. You can't study erratically or occasionally. It just doesn't work. You have to be in the right mindset to study properly. Think about it. What are you doing when you study? You are trying to cram as much information into your mind as you can. That won't lead to success. Instead, spread it out into reasonable chucks and stay dedicated to your study schedule so that you can get all the necessary information in.

If you need a visual example, below is a study schedule that can work for anyone no matter their situation in life. Take this schedule and modify it so that it can fit your lifestyle and personal preferences perfectly. Your schedule should look like this:

- Monday to Friday: study for two hours in the evening
- Saturdays: study for four hours during the day
- Sunday: full break; no studying

Throw out any distractions. Barring matters of life and death, don't let anything keep you away from those goals. You might not think so, but there are rarely any distractions worth taking you away from your studies.

There are two basic kinds of distractions. There is a distraction that keeps you from studying altogether, and there are other distractions that simply interrupt you. Let's look at some examples of the two different kinds.

TV is a common distraction. If you decide to "delay" your studying to finish an episode of your favorite show, you could easily end up not studying at all. If you are actively studying, things like YouTube videos or visiting friends can also interrupt and distract you from the goals you had that day. Take the time to find out what your distractions are. Then, get rid of them. Having distractions can derail you from your study routines, and that will make your total studying time even longer because you are not taking advantage of the time you have already set aside to learn. During study times, make sure to study the entire time. Allow yourself only short, scheduled breaks.

Find a quiet study place that you feel comfortable in. This should be an area where no one will bother you. It shouldn't be anywhere you do anything else. Try your hardest to find a dedicated space just for studying. It will help you keep a schedule and stay focused. It can also signal to your family and friends that this is your studying time and you need to be left alone. Simply going to this study place can also be enough to get your mind prepared for studying. This space should ideally not have a TV set or any other distractions, like your phone. If you're using a computer, only look at the online resources you need to study—absolutely no Twitter, Facebook, YouTube, or any other time-eaters.

Don't be afraid to take study breaks. You cannot study all day, and doing so will make you become inefficient. Use your time in the best way. The longer you study, the more likely it will be for you to get distracted. Taking a 10-minute break every hour or two can relieve your mind and help you feel better and more energized. Be sure to keep it short or you could find yourself unable to refocus and get motivated again.

Breaks let your mind rest and store the information that you have just taken in. It allows you to take in more information at a later time. Again, don't take a very long break. This is the time to rest or have a snack—not to find a million distractions.

You have to prepare your mind for studying. Before you start a study session, take a couple of minutes to get yourself mentally prepared for the challenge. Turn off the distractions and get focused. Take a few deep breaths to clear your head of everything else going on in your life and put your whole being into your studies.

When you are doing something difficult like studying for the CPA, you can find yourself really distracted by things that are a total waste of time and energy. Just because you are sitting at your desk for two hours, doesn't mean you are actually studying. You could just as easily be off somewhere else in your mind. There is no need to waste time. After seriously focusing on your studies, you can just go on and reward yourself by doing other things.

Chapter 20: Preparing for Test Day

If you are considering which test to study for, know first that there are plenty of options. Here, we'll give you our best recommendations.

The FAR exam can be a great place to start. It actually covers more information than any other part. It can be overwhelming, but if you can make it through this one, the others will feel less challenging. Choosing this exam has another advantage; that is, many of the basic concepts in other exams will be touched on in the FAR exam. Studying for this section will help you build your information base and finish the exam's entirety successfully.

To prepare for the test day, make sure to write out a schedule on how to most effectively take your exam. Write how long each test will take you to complete and use that schedule to keep yourself on track during the important day.

The AUD (Auditing and Attestation) section of the exam is often taken earlier than other parts of the exam, but you can do what you think will work best for you. You have four hours to take it, and you will have five sub-tests to get through. It is a computerized test that will escalate in difficulty based on how well you are doing. Start from the total hours and count *down*. Here is an example:

Testlet 1 – 4:00 down to 3:15 (45 minutes)

Testlet 2 – 3:15 down to 2:30 (45 minutes)

Testlet 3 – 2:30 down to 2:00 (30 minutes)

Break – 15 minute

Testlet 4 – 2:00 down to 1:00 (1 hour)

Testlet 5 – 1:00 to 0:00 (1 hour)

If you make a list of your time, you can have a more concrete idea of the duration in which to complete each testlet and gauge your speed. After all, answering every question is incredibly important. Planning your time can help give you the chance to answer everything and increase your probability of success.

Chapter 21: A Typical Day-to-Day of a Forensic Accountant

Forensic accountants are hired to interpret and present complex information and financial and business matters in a way that can be easily understood and proven. Forensic accountants are everywhere: public practice, government agencies, even police forces. They are basically in every kind of organization.

Forensic accountants are involved in many different jobs every day, and conducting investigations is a huge part of their job. They also develop tech applications to assist with financial analysis and presentation of evidence. Forms and documentation are essential elements of forensic accounting.

The working conditions are different depending on your firm and position. Most work a typical 9-to-5 day in offices. They typically work about 40 hours per week, Monday to Friday, but over time may be needed on occasion. You can work for businesses, financial institutions, and organizations like insurance companies. There can be teamwork with co-workers and other investigators.

The daily routine of a forensic accountant is a diverse one. A forensic accountant follows assignments, so their daily routines will be drastically different depending on the firm they work for. They may simply go over the company's financial record on a particular day. On another day, they may conduct a fraud investigation with employee interviews. There will never be a set routine for any forensic accountant. Every day will be a fresh one with something brand new to do. The skills you will need will be just as diverse.

Chapter 22: Becoming a Certified Fraud Examiner

As you do your research on forensic accounting, you may come across a special certification called a Certified Fraud Examiner.

As you know, fraud is any deceptive acts done intentionally for personal gain. A certified fraud examiner is a professional who is very knowledgeable and qualified in all levels of fraud investigation, both civil and criminal. There are many types of fraud, and they come in all sorts of forms. Some examples include payroll fraud, embezzlement, and skimming. Every business has dealt with fraud in some way whether it was reported or not. A certified fraud examiner has to use their knowledge of complex transactions, law, and fraud techniques to solve these cases.

The duties of a certified fraud examiner come in three parts. These include conducting interviews, finding fraud sources and writing reports, and identifying the risk for fraud in business. A certified fraud examiner has to be proactive in evaluating the fraud risk. They will need to identify evidence of fraud and organize it in a manner that's easy to understand. The types of information that may be gathered include billing information, financial data, and financial relationships. They might interview witnesses and include their statements in the documentation.

Typically, a certified fraud examiner will testify in court about any fraud allegations. They might also work as analysts for law enforcement and lawyers dealing with people charged with fraud. Many certified fraud examiners help organizations organize fraud detection and prevention efforts. They might also design and maintain internal controls like fraud prevention and detection methods.

To become a certified fraud examiner, the first thing you need to have is a bachelor's degree, but as a forensic accountant, you would already have that. The next thing you will need to do is to get a passing score on the Association of Certified Fraud Examiners. This certification is comprehensive, and the only place to get certified as a fraud examiner is at the ACFE.

Getting the certification is only the first step. You will need to maintain the certification you have earned and complete 20 or more hours of professional education every year. You will be responsible for keeping up your knowledge of trends and current events in fraud activities. Your knowledge will need to be thorough and extensive, but your skills can't end there. Just like forensic accountants, to be effective in your job, you also need soft skills such as an excellent interpersonal communication. An important part of your job is to carefully listen to people so that you can glean if they are being honest about any potential fraud. You also need to have financial skills and business sense to be able to quickly identify inaccurate or fraudulent information.

The projected career outlook for a certified fraud examiner is one that will continue to be positive. Fraud is a nationwide problem that continues to worsen over time. It costs people over $600 billion in just the USA alone. All around the world, the figures are four to five times that. Certified fraud examiners are very much in demand and will continue to be so. The desire to meditate risk is constantly increasing, after all, and it makes a lot of sense that there will be a 10% rise in the hiring of fraud examiners by 2024.

A certified fraud examiner has to have a completely unique set of skills. They need to be someone who can do what no ordinary accountant can. In today's world, there are so many tools that criminals can use to enable financial deception. The faster the world goes, the easier it is for criminals to get one over unsuspecting citizens. That is one reason for the rate of fraud being so alarming.

This is what keeps the field of forensic accounting pushing forward. As long as there are people trying to take advantage of the system, there will be a need for people who can protect its weaknesses from being exploited. This is a diverse and exciting field of accounting. Every day could be an entirely new one. Who doesn't want a dynamic and exciting career in a field that is stable and has such a positive outlook? Plus, you can make a real difference in the life of other people. This is the kind of job that can help the world in positive ways.

Conclusion

Fraud is a growing concern that lawyers, law enforcement, forensic accountants, and detectives battle every day. The enemy is not the people who commit the crime; it is technology. The same tools that are used to fight crime, criminals use to steal from companies and organizations. Moreover, technology will only continue to advance, so we need to as well.

Several jobs require a forensic accountant. If there is a job or company that wants to see success, then a forensic accountant can be used. The point is that they are in high demand. The skills they hold are not easy to obtain. It takes a lifetime of education, and it does not stop upon receiving your degree. As new types of fraud come into existence, more training is needed to find out how to combat new issues.

The specific skills listed in chapter 2 will help you get started on the path to becoming a forensic accountant. Remember, you are the expert, and there will be times that forensic accounting is not effective, and times you need to accept defeat and rely on others to help solve a case.

Each person in an investigation plays an important role to crack the case open and bring about justice. Fraud is a serious crime and causes huge corporations to collapse and crumble.

Do not think you know the answer to every question or situation. Some cases will be open and shut while others may take months or years to nut out. Do the research; know all the tools that are available to you and keep up-to-date on new cases that hit the news. Just like in chapter 10, there is a lot to learn about past cases.

You have been given all the tools and resources you need. Now you are on your way to becoming the next 'Sherlock Holmes' – well, of the forensic accounting world anyway.

Good luck, detective!

Check out more books by Greg Shields

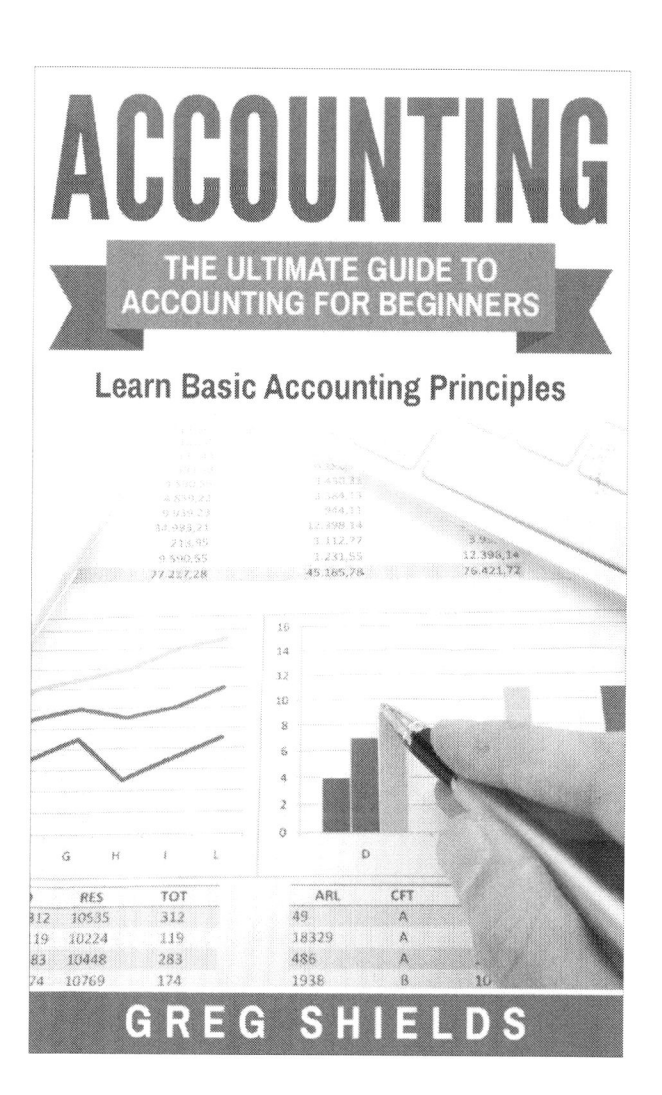

ACCOUNTING

THE ULTIMATE GUIDE TO ACCOUNTING FOR BEGINNERS

Learn Basic Accounting Principles

GREG SHIELDS

BOOKKEEPING

THE ULTIMATE GUIDE TO BOOKKEEPING FOR SMALL BUSINESS

GREG SHIELDS

FINANCIAL STATEMENTS

THE ULTIMATE GUIDE TO FINANCIAL STATEMENT ANALYSIS FOR BUSINESS OWNERS AND INVESTORS

GREG SHIELDS

Printed in Great Britain
by Amazon